INTEGRATION AND COMMUNITY BUILDING
IN EASTERN EUROPE

INTEGRATION AND COMMUNITY BUILDING
IN EASTERN EUROPE

Jan F. Triska, series editor

The German Democratic Republic

Arthur M. Hanhardt, Jr.

The Polish People's Republic

James F. Morrison

The Development of Socialist Yugoslavia

M. George Zaninovich

The People's Republic of Albania

Nicholas C. Pano

THE POLISH PEOPLE'S REPUBLIC

THE
POLISH
PEOPLE'S
REPUBLIC

JAMES F. MORRISON

THE JOHNS HOPKINS PRESS

Baltimore

FOREWORD

The *Polish People's Republic* is part of a series of monographs dealing with integration and community building in the communist party states of eastern Europe. These monographs are further part of a larger program of studies of the communist system sponsored by Stanford University.

It seems appropriate here to outline the theoretical and methodological concepts that were developed for the series as a whole. The focus has been on the communist-ruled states as part of a loosely structured community or system—its origins, development, and internal behavior. The major underlying assumption is that each communist party state has characteristics peculiar to it that predispose it toward varying degrees of co-operation, co-ordination, and integration with the others. We think that the present behavioral characteristics of the system can be traced to environmental, attitudinal, and systemic factors, and that we can learn a great deal from a comparative analysis of the process and degree of integration of each member state into the community of communist party states—whether, for example, the process involves force or consent, similar or shared institutions and codes of behavior, or whether integration is effective at elite levels and/or at lower levels as well, and so on.

The concept of political integration and community formation and maintenance is, as a focus of intellectual curiosity and investigation, as old as the study of politics. The mushrooming of supranational integrational movements since World War II has given a considerable new impetus to the old curiosity and has changed the emphasis of the investigations. Social scientists, who in the last two decades have been building a general theory of political integration, whether on a subnational, national, or supranational level, have been perhaps less concerned with the philosophical content of the concept of integration than with discovering operational indicators that would endow the concept with empirical meaning and allow the theory to be tested for validity and reliability. The principal centers of their inquiry have been two broad independent variables, *interaction* and *attitude*. Although in most cases investigated separately, interaction and attitude are assumed to combine to constitute a community, the objective of the process of integration.

The principal subjects of inquiry have been transactions across the boundaries of states and attitude formation within them. The theorists stipulate that the number and density of transactions among states indicate the degree and nature of their relationships. Flow of mail and telephone traffic; trade; aid; exchange of tourists, officials, and migrants; cultural exchange of persons and communications; newspapers, periodicals, and book sales and translations; radio, TV, and motion picture exchange; mutual treaties and agreements; and common organizations and conferences are the kinds of indicators that, measured and plotted over time, should demonstrate the direction of integrational trends and developments.

With reference to attitude formation, theorists have been more concerned with the process of integration than with its results (conditions) within states. The pertinent literature yields relatively little on this subject. In *Nationalism and Social Communication,* Karl Deutsch argues that it may be fruitful to study two sets of persons within a unit of analysis: those "mobilized" for integrational communications and those "assimilated" into the new, larger unit. If those assimilated multiply at a more rapid rate than those mobilized, then "assimilation" is gaining and "community is growing faster than society."

At present enormous problems are involved in studying the results of the integration process in communist countries. It is difficult to assess attitudes because of the great sensitivity of officials and decision makers, and it is either difficult or impossible to obtain reliable aggregate and survey data. This informational problem makes it correspondingly difficult to develop a general theory of integration or to make systematic comparative analyses. We have therefore been compelled to rely on indicators of degrees and trends, a method that depends considerably on subjective judgment and inference.

Although the data available are uneven in quality and quantity, our approach has been rigorous and systematic. Each author was asked to examine the country under review with reference to five historical periods: (1) the precommunist stage before the country became a party state and hence a member of the system; (2) the period of the communists' consolidation of power after World War II when the states of eastern Europe entered the system; (3) the subsequent era of repression and rigid controls; (4) the period of relaxed controls following Stalin's death; (5) the last ten years. For each of these periods, as appropriate, the author was asked to identify and analyze the phenomena relevant to his country's integration in the system: its ecological-physical features, its demographic structure, belief system, social system, degree of autonomy, its dependence on other states, and its hopes, needs, and expectations with regard to integration and development. Within these broad confines, each author was asked to emphasize the periods and events with the greatest significance for the integrational development of the country in question. It is our feeling that a more rigid set of prescriptions would have been self-defeating in view of our objectives and the exploratory nature of our undertaking.

Like the other monographs in the series, this study is divided into five historical parts. Each period is discussed in terms of the changes that took place in the environment of the Polish socioeconomic–political system—both in other parts of the communist system and in the rest of the world—and is analyzed for the most significant domestic changes relevant to Poland's integration into the system. In addition, there is a discussion in each period of the changes that took place in the form and degree of Poland's integration with the system, the costs and benefits for various segments of the Polish population, and the major conflicts between Poland and the rest of the system resulting from the nature of the integration during the given period.

One final remark of a general nature is in order. The series is based on the assumption that although the countries of eastern Europe are now gaining more freedom to conduct their own affairs, they do not reject the need for association among themselves as such. All the communist parties in power in eastern Europe find real and necessary the idea of a world communist community united in opposing capitalism and in carrying out its historical destiny. All of them, we believe, would find it instinctively repugnant to do anything that could precipitate a final, total break with the communist system.

This series is an intellectual product of many creative minds. In addition to the authors of the individual monographs—in this case, Professor James F. Morrison, Department of Political Science, University of Florida—I would like to thank especially Professor David D. Finley of The Colorado College and Stanford University for his original contribution and assistance.

JAN F. TRISKA

Institute of Political Studies
Stanford University

CONTENTS

INTRODUCTION

Nearly a quarter of a century has now passed since Poland became a member of the communist system in the wake of the Red Army's great push westward toward Berlin during the closing days of World War II. Indisputable Soviet military domination of the area, a war-weary and acquiescent West, the internal chaos left in Poland by years of war and occupation, six million dead, and enormous wartime destruction made it possible for the Soviet Union—determined to protect its western frontier—to bring to power a handful of Polish communists and sympathizers. With Soviet guidance and assistance and through skillful political maneuvering, they were able in the course of the next decade to transform almost completely the existing internal political and economic systems and to effect Poland's integration into the international communist system. This integration has not been complete, however, nor has its form remained the same. It is the purpose of this study to explore in a general way the extent to which Poland has become integrated into the communist world and to suggest how and why the forms of the integration have changed over the years.

It seems particularly useful to study Poland and its integration into the communist world because of the country's historical and contemporary importance. Poland first emerged as a distinct political system in the middle of the tenth century and soon became one of the most important and powerful states in central Europe, playing a particularly significant role in the history of the region between the fourteenth and seventeenth centuries after the voluntary integration of Poland and Lithuania which resulted eventually in the unification of the once separate political and economic systems.[1]

Despite the development of a rich and distinctive culture and often spectacular political fortunes, Poland was almost continually plagued with problems of internal disunity and numerous challenges from its often strong and aggressive neighbors, especially the Germans, Tartars, Turks, and Swedes. Finally, in the late eighteenth century Poland had its first experience with forced integration as Prussia (later Ger-

[1]For general background reading on Poland see the following:
General history—Oscar Halecki, *History of Poland,* trans. Monica Gardner and Mary Corbridge-Patkaniowska (New York: Roy Publishers, 1956); William F. Reddaway *et al.,* eds., *The Cambridge History of Poland,* 2 vols. (Cambridge: Cambridge U. Press, 1941, 1950).
General handbooks—Clifford R. Barnett, *Poland: Its People, Society, and Culture* (New Haven: Hraf Press, 1958); Oscar Halecki, ed., *Poland* (New York: Praeger, 1957); and Alicja Iwanska, *Contemporary Poland* (University of Chicago for the Human Relations Area Files, 1955).
Pre-entry period history—Hans Roos, *A History of Modern Poland,* trans. J. R. Foster (New York: Knopf, 1966); Robert Machray, *The Poland of Pilsudski, 1914–1936* (New York: Dutton, 1957); Stanislaw Mackiewicz, *Historia Polski od 11 Listopada 1918r. do 17 Wrzesnia 1939r.* (London, 1941); and Ferdynand Zweig, *Poland Between Two Wars: A Critical Study of Social and Economic Changes* (London: Secker and Warburg, 1944).

many), Russia, and Austria, taking advantage of Poland's internal weaknesses, eliminated the Polish state from the map of Europe in three successive partitions of its territory. During the century and a quarter of occupation which followed, Polish nationalism and unity were kept alive and even strengthened by the great productivity of patriotic writers, artists, and musicians living and working abroad in exile, by the activities of intellectuals and patriots at home, and by the Polish Catholic church. Because of these factors, Poland had been integrated economically and administratively with the three occupying powers—with important consequences for Poland's subsequent development—but never developed a sense of community with any of them.

After the restoration of the Polish state following World War I, the Poles asserted their independence even more strongly than before. It was difficult to cooperate closely with any of their neighbors and impossible to adopt any major integration scheme. World War II, however, involved Poland in its second major encounter with forced integration; the Germans and the Russians divided Poland between them, each absorbing part of the Polish territory and population into its own political system. The Soviet Union effectively integrated the segment it absorbed and still retains control of this area today—though the Polish part of the population was allowed to emigrate to Poland at various times after the war. The Germans divided their territory into two parts. One part they incorporated into Germany proper; the other part became the so-called General Government, or occupied Poland. A strong resistance developed in the German-occupied parts of Poland, and the war ended before the Germans could make the integration effective in other than a superficial military and economic sense.

The end of the war brought the third major Polish encounter with forced integration—this time with the communist system. Now, almost 25 years later, after many changes both in Poland and in the operation of the system, Poland for the first time in its 1,000-year history seems to be effectively and permanently integrated to a significant degree into a larger political system—a system for which, interestingly enough, many of its own nationals, such as Rosa Luxemburg and Felix Dzierdzinski, helped lay the foundations in the nineteenth and early twentieth centuries. The present Polish elite seems to be playing an increasingly important role in the further development of the communist system, especially of its eastern European member states. Poland has also become one of the most important members of the system in other ways. It is the third largest communist-ruled state in population (after China and the U.S.S.R.), fourth largest in land area (after the U.S.S.R., China, and Mongolia), fifth in Party membership (after China, the U.S.S.R., Czechoslovakia, and the G.D.R.), fourth in per capita gross national product (after the U.S.S.R., Czechoslovakia, and the G.D.R.), and potentially the third most important in industrial production (it is already third in crude steel production and energy consumption—after the U.S.S.R. and China). Because of its strategic location between the U.S.S.R. and Germany, Poland is also of importance to the system and must continue to play a key part in any strategic considerations.

The Polish Communist Party leadership has played a growing part in system-wide affairs, and after the Sino-Soviet split has probably been second in importance to the Soviet leadership itself. The Party leadership has been a force for tolerance of diversity in domestic affairs within a context of system unity and co-operation.

In 1956 Poland played one of the most important parts in initiating the move toward greater diversity within the communist world and put most emphasis on the importance of sovereign equality of each member state, asserting its independence in what was then considered by most observers—both inside and outside the system—to be a rebellious and highly independent move that could not help but weaken the system. Yet historians of the future may conclude that Poland, on the contrary, has proven to be one of the most important integrators, conciliators, and builders of a new and more viable association of communist states; by promoting a greater degree of decentralization and participation by all the eastern European member states, Poland helped to lay the foundation for a more stable and lasting integration. In short, the Poles seem to have contributed to a move toward integration at a new and somewhat lower level of equilibrium, allowing for less centralized control, the assertion of national interests as interpreted by nationally oriented ruling communist elites, and a less exclusive economic and political integration with the communist world. The increase in trade and other forms of co-operation with noncommunist states has reduced the costs of integration, making the communist system more stable and viable.

Although the basic research for this monograph was done primarily in the United States, I also gained many insights of great value in preparing it during the two years I spent in Poland on the Stanford-Warsaw Graduate Exchange Program in 1960–61 and 1964–65. I am indebted to Stanford University for making it possible for me to spend this time in Poland and to the many Poles—both friends and total strangers—who contributed in an indirect way to this project, though neither they nor I knew at the time the extent to which they were helping me understand their culture and social system. I am greatly indebted to Professor Jan F. Triska, who originally suggested this project and encouraged me to write about Poland and the international communist system. I am also grateful to the several friends and colleagues who read this manuscript in its many stages of development and who offered their helpful criticisms and suggestions.

JAMES F. MORRISON

Department of Political Science
University of Florida

GENERAL INFORMATION

The Polish alphabet is the Latin alphabet with a few additions. These letters and the letters the pronunciation of which differs from their pronunciation in English are listed below:

Polish Letter	Approximate English Equivalent
ą	nasal as in French "bon"
c	ts (wi*ts*)
cz	ch (*ch*ur*ch*); palatalized
ć	ch (*ch*ur*ch*); softer than cz
dz	dz (a*dz*e)
dż	g (*g*entleman)
dź	dg (sle*dg*e)
ę	nasal, as in French "fin"
ch	h strongly aspirated (Scotch lo*ch*)
i	ee (m*ee*t)
j	y (*y*es)
ł	w (*w*ater); in literary Polish, l (cand*l*e)
ń	soft n (*n*ew)
ó	long o (m*oo*se)
r	hard, trilling r
rz	s (mea*s*ure)
ś	sh (*sh*ore); palatalized
sz	sh (*sh*op)
u	oo (m*oo*se)
w	v (*v*ine)
y	short i (p*i*n)
ż	soft s (mea*s*ure)
ź	soft z (azure)

The Polish People's Republic (P.P.R.)
Polska Rzeczpospolita Ludowa

Area: 312,520 sq. km.

Population: 31,811,000 (1966 est.)

Density: 102 per sq. km. 50% urban (1966 est.)

Major cities:	Population: (1966 est.)
Warsaw	1,267,800
Lodz	746,500
Cracow	530,400
Poznan	442,500
Gdansk	326,800
Wroclaw	480,600

Birth rate: 16.7 per 1000 (1966 est.)

Death rate: 7.3 per 1000 (1966 est.)

Infant mortality: 38.6 per 1000 (1966 est.)

Marriages: 7.1 per 1000 (1966 est.)

Emigration: 28,755 (1966)

Population growth rate: 9.4 per 1000 (1966 est.)

School enrollment (1966/67) in thousands: Pre-school, 470; elementary, 5,527; secondary, 322; special, 66; vocational, 629; higher education, 274; adult education, 180

Illiteracy (7 years and older): 2.7% (1960)

Newspapers and periodicals (1966)
   Titles: 1,418; copies printed, 2,565 million

Public libraries: 8,198 (1966)

Radio receivers: 5,593,000 (1966)

TV receivers: 2,540,000 (1966)

Cinemas: 3,836 (1966)

Communications network:
   Hard-surface roads: 119,409 km
   Railroads: 26,739 km
   Airlines (domestic): 3,557 km
   Waterways: 6,855 km

Currency: Polish zloty   *Metric system*

The Polish People's Republic

1: POLAND IN THE PRE-ENTRY PERIOD, 1918–39

The Pre-Entry Environment[1]

The military and diplomatic events of the World War I period had four major effects on Poland. First, Poland's independence was restored after well over a century of partition and occupation.[2] Second, independence revived Poland's historic problem of being a relatively small and weak state surrounded by more powerful neighbors interested in expanding their territory.[3] Third, Poland's eastern neighbor underwent a profound revolution that soon made the U.S.S.R. not only an increasingly powerful potential military threat, but also the nucleus of an embryonic, world-wide, revolutionary political system, whose leaders predicted that Poland, too, soon would be absorbed by the new system and transformed into a communist society. Fourth, the same peace settlement that restored

[1]For the purpose of this analysis of Poland, the pre-entry period began with the restoration of its independence at the end of World War I and ended with the beginning of World War II when events began to move more swiftly and decisively to bring Poland into the communist system. Except where necessary to explain later developments, the pre-entry description concentrates on the one year and eight months immediately before the German invasion of Poland on September 1, 1939.

[2]For a history of this period see: Titus Komarnicki, *Rebirth of the Polish Republic: A Study in the Diplomatic History of Europe, 1914–1921* (London: Heinemann, 1957).

[3]The Austrian Empire had ceased to be a threat, but Germany and the U.S.S.R. remained. Poland was of particular interest to the latter because it was located on what was historically the main invasion route from the West to Russia.

Poland's independence and temporarily reduced the German military threat also ironically contributed substantially to the rise of Hitler and an aggressive German foreign policy that finally triggered World War II and the chain of events which eventually brought Poland into the communist system.

In addition to the fact that Poland was located in a strategically disadvantageous position between two traditionally hostile world powers, there were other disadvantages to Poland's geographical position. Most important of these was that there were no natural or man-made barriers to aid in the defense of Poland's extensive borders with Germany, East Prussia, or the U.S.S.R. Poland also shared relatively short borders with Rumania on the south and with Latvia, Lithuania, and the Free City of Danzig on the north.

It is worth noting that nearly all of Poland's frontier bordered on states with which it had poor relations. Poland had not only been involved in serious disputes with its most important traditional enemies, Germany and Russia—having even waged a major war with the latter after the end of World War I—but its potential allies, Lithuania and Czechoslovakia, had also been alienated by border disputes. The only ally with which Poland shared a common border was relatively weak Rumania (mutual defense treaty, 1921). Poland was geographically isolated from France, its major ally (treaty of consultation, 1921; military convention, 1922), and from any other state that could be expected to aid meaningfully in its defense in the event of an armed attack.[4]

[4]For example, once its deterrent effect had failed, the March, 1939, declaration by Great Britain that it would assist Poland if the latter were attacked was rendered almost meaningless as far as the defense of Poland was concerned because of the geographical distance that separated the two states.

Poland's only outlet to the sea was a short, 140 kilo-meter strip of the Baltic seacoast (half of it on the narrow Hel Peninsula).[5] Access to the sea was still not really secure, however, because of the predominantly German population of Danzig and the consequent *de facto* German control of the port and the mouth of the Vistula River. To remedy the situation the Poles built their own great port of Gdynia to which they had rail and road access through the corridor.

Demographic Structure

By 1939 the Polish population of 34.8 million[6] was still largely concentrated in the rural areas.[7] Industrial-ization was, however, gradually decreasing the propor-tion of the rural population, though not its absolute numbers.[8] Between 1936 and 1938 the population was increasing at an average annual rate of 11.2 per thou-sand, with a birth rate of 25.3.[9]

The prewar Polish population included a high pro-portion of minority groups, a fact which created a great

[5] The postwar peace agreements had restored Poland's access to the sea through a narrow corridor of once Polish land be-tween Germany proper and East Prussia. This land, though still largely Polish in population outside the cities, had been under German control for centuries.

[6] The last prewar census was made in 1931 and indicated a population of 32,107,000. *Concise Statistical Yearbook of Po-land, 1938,* p. 12.

[7] In 1931 72.8 per cent of the population lived in rural areas with 60.5 per cent of the population dependent on agriculture for their income. *Statistical Yearbook of Poland, 1938,* pp. 12, 30.

[8] In 1931, when the last prewar census was made, only 27.2 per cent of the population lived in urban areas (*Rocznik Staty-styczny, 1959,* p. 20). This was an increase from 24 per cent in 1921 and 20 per cent in 1900 (*Concise Statistical Yearbook of Poland, 1938,* p. 19).

[9] *Rocznik Statystyczny, 1959,* p. 25.

deal of trouble for Poland; both domestically and with its neighbors.[10] Only about 70 per cent of the population was ethnically Polish. The Ukrainians, who numbered over 4 million, were the largest minority group.[11] The Jewish population of Poland numbered 3.35 million, or roughly 10 per cent of the population.[12] There were also nearly 2 million Belorussians, living mostly on the poor land of the east; 741,000 Germans (1931 census, based on mother tongue); 138,700 Russians (1931); 38,000 Czechs and Slovaks (1931 estimate); 84,000 Lithuanians, most of whom lived in Wilno province (1931); an unknown number of gypsies (perhaps 30,000-50,000); and a variety of other small minority groups.[13]

The languages spoken in Poland corresponded roughly to the ethnic group patterns, though an increasing proportion of each group spoke Polish, the

[10]See also: Stephen Horek, *Poland and Her National Minorities, 1919–1939* (New York: Vintage Press, 1961).

[11]They lived primarily in the southeastern part of Poland, which had been under Polish rule for centuries. Though the Ukrainians often constituted a clear majority outside the cities and towns, the Polish population controlled the land and the economy.

[12]Before the seventeenth century Poland had been a haven for the Jews, who, persecuted elsewhere in Europe, came to Poland where they were allowed to develop a near monopoly in trade, banking, and merchandising until the end of serfdom in Poland in the nineteenth century. In the interwar period most of the Jewish population was concentrated in settlements, but perhaps 15 per cent were assimilated into Polish culture to the point where they could be classified as speaking Polish as their mother tongue. (According to the 1931 census, 371,900 of the 3,113,900 Jews were in the Polish-speaking category. *Concise Statistical Yearbook of Poland, 1938*, p. 26.)

[13]These figures should be considered only rough approximations as there is always disagreement about how nationality is to be defined. Germany, for example, claimed that there were over 1.7 million Germans in Poland between the wars.

official and dominant language.[14] The more important minority groups, however, often had their own schools and taught in their own language,[15] a right guaranteed by the Minorities Treaty of 1919 and the Constitution of 1921.

About 95 per cent of the Polish part of the population was Roman Catholic, but approximately 35 per cent of the total population followed other faiths. In addition to the Jewish population,[16] most of the other ethnic minorities were also set off from the Polish population by religious differences.[17] Most of the Russians and Belorussians were Russian Orthodox, the largest religious minority (3.76 million adherents in 1931). The Ukrainians were divided between the Russian Orthodox faith and the Uniate faith (which observed the Greek Catholic traditions—with 3.34 million adherents in 1931). Most of the Germans were Lutherans. Only the Czechs and Lithuanians shared the Poles' Roman Catholic faith.

It is worth emphasizing that the Roman Catholic faith of the Polish population not only intensified the cleavage at home between the Polish and non-Polish parts of the population, but also tended to set them

[14]In fact the ethnic group estimates given here are based on the 1931 census, which used mother tongue as the basis for classification and, consequently, probably underestimate the size of most ethnic minorities. It is probably a fairly accurate measure of the existing cultural minorities, however.

[15]For a breakdown of the Polish schools according to the language of instruction see: *Concise Statistical Yearbook of Poland, 1938,* p. 310.

[16]The estimate of the Jewish minority here is based on the census figures of 1931 which apparently used religion as the basis of classification. Therefore, virtually all those classified above as ethnically Jewish also followed the Jewish religion.

[17]For a table comparing religion and mother tongue see: *Concise Statistical Yearbook of Poland, 1938,* p. 26.

off from their traditional enemies, the Russians (Russian Orthodox) and the Germans and Swedes (Protestant). The atheism of the Soviet government further increased the religious difference between the two societies.

The Belief System[18]

The dominant belief system in Poland was that of the aristocracy and middle class. It tended to pervade the urban areas (particularly the cultural centers of Cracow, Vilno, Lvov, and Warsaw) and, because most government officials came from the middle-class, urban, or aristocratic groups, whose dominant belief system also characterized the Polish pre-entry government. The nucleus of this thought emphasized individualism, romanticism, social formality, Polish nationalism and patriotism, Catholicism, and the Western cultural heritage. It stressed great respect for the fine arts, science and scholarship, and intense pride in the great Polish scientists and artists of the past: Copernicus, Chopin, Madame Curie, Mickiewicz, Sienkiewicz, and so forth. At the same time it included a strong, fundamental dislike of authority of any kind.

The Polish identification of the individual with the nation was strong and idealized, though perhaps more in a romantic than a practical, everyday sense. The emphasis on individualism and the distaste for authority made joint effort difficult at the national level and discouraged the development of a strong individual sense

[18]The Polish pre-entry belief system is analyzed here by first considering the dominant belief system of the aristocracy and middle class and then discussing the politically relevant differences to be found in the belief systems of the peasants and the urban workers.

of social responsibility. In contrast to this attitude toward everyday affairs, when the nation was threatened from without the situation evoked an uncompromising attitude and great personal and national heroism.[19]

The Polish Catholic church also was closely associated with the concept of an independent Polish nation, an attitude that had its roots deep in Polish history.[20] Furthermore, it directed the Polish cultural orientation toward the West. Latin monks brought much from the West to Poland in the early years of the state's development and later provided an important link with cultural developments in western Europe. The Roman Catholic Church played only a minor part in the spread of tradition, however, since the Polish Catholic church had a peculiarly national character and did little to identify the Poles with other Catholic nations.

[19]In some circles it was even believed that Poland had a special place among nations and that its role, like that sometimes attributed to the Jew among men, was to be the suffering servant whose sacrifices would help redeem the world.

[20]The close relationship between the Church and the nation had begun when Poland's first king accepted Roman Catholicism and converted the nation to his faith. In addition, the Church had also played an important role in both politics and cultural developments during the early centuries of the Polish state. During the period of the great partitions and occupation, the Church provided the only organized link that united the Polish nation, doing much to preserve the Polish language and culture in the face of attempts to destroy it made by the occupying powers. The identification of Poland with the Catholic church was further strengthened by the fact that its major enemies—the Germans, the Swedes, and the Russians, not to mention the Mongols and the Tartars—had been of different religious faiths. At the same time, however, it is important to note that there was considerable anticlerical feeling in Poland, particularly among the intelligentsia. Likewise, the ethnic and religious minorities did not share the Poles' feeling about the Roman Catholic church.

The lack of a language in common with their neighbors also helped reinforce the Poles' fundamental feeling of separateness. The common Slavic background of the Poles, Russians, Ukrainians, Czechs, and Slovaks was offset by the traditional conflicts between Poland and the other Slavic states.

Cultural ties with the West—particularly with France—were strengthened after the partitions of the late eighteenth century. During Napoleon's great march to the east, an independent Poland allied with France was set up briefly, and the door was opened even further to widespread French cultural influence, including the introduction of a legal system based on the Napoleonic Code. After Napoleon's defeat, Polish attempts to regain independence aroused much sympathy in France. Many Polish intellectuals and artists, including Chopin, went to France and elsewhere in the West to work in exile.

Although Western ties were further strengthened by a great Polish immigration to America in the late nineteenth and early twentieth centuries and by the part that Woodrow Wilson played in the restoration of Polish independence at the end of World War I,[21] it was undoubtedly with France that the Poles continued to identify most closely. This attitude toward France was reinforced during the pre-entry period by the fact that France was pursuing an active policy of trying to maintain and strengthen the Polish position as an ally and counterweight to German and bolshevik power in central Europe.[22] A French loan late in the

[21]See also: John W. Kimball, "The U.S. and Poland between the Two Wars" (M.A. thesis, Stanford University, 1961).

[22]See also: P. S. Wandycz, *France and Her Eastern Allies* (Minneapolis: U. of Minnesota Press, 1962).

pre-entry period was also a great help to the Polish economy.

At the same time, Poland's history and culture were different enough from those of its neighbors—and nationalistic enough—to prevent any sense of close identification with any particular state. Even the identification with distant France was never really profound for most Poles and seems to have developed more out of admiration than from similarity. Although Poland's culture and institutions were different from those of her neighbors, they were in and of themselves no cause for conflict with any state except the U.S.S.R., which for ideological reasons could not be expected to accept Poland as a friendly neighbor as long as the latter maintained its prewar socioeconomic system and its feudal–bourgeois cultural outlook. The growing difference between Polish and Soviet cultural institutions in the interwar period probably further decreased the amount of Polish identification with its eastern neighbor, though it is undoubtedly true that the minority of communists, socialists, and other political groups on the left looked more sympathetically on the Soviet experiment than did the government and the majority of the Polish population.

As a result of the geographic, demographic, and cultural factors outlined above, the Poles during the pre-entry period perceived themselves as being a unique and separate nation, surrounded by culturally different and unfriendly states, geographically isolated from their friends, and in need of defending themselves against their potential enemies, especially the U.S.S.R. and Germany. They also saw themselves in the light of their former position as a world power and aspired to regain some of their past greatness.

After World War I the Poles consequently structured their initial foreign policy goal toward reestablishing the Polish state and expanding its borders to encompass as much of its former territory as possible in the cases where the peace settlements imposed by the allies did not fully accord with Polish demands. Despite initial postwar successes against Lithuania and the U.S.S.R., however, it soon became clear that because of Poland's relatively weak position in relation to its neighbors there was little hope that its territory could be expanded much beyond what had already been achieved.[23] For the rest of the interwar period the major Polish foreign policy goal was defensive in character, aimed at preserving Poland's security and independence from Germany and the Soviet Union.

Immediately after the war the Poles worried primarily about the advance of bolshevism. Increasingly, however—especially after the rise of Hitler—the government became concerned about the German threat in view of the weakness of France and the growing German demands for a revision of her eastern boundaries at Poland's expense.

The failure to build a federation or alliance of central European states at the end of World War I— which had been proposed by Pilsudski and others as the answer to Poland's problem of defense against its traditional enemies[24]—and the subsequent ineffective-

[23]At the Munich Conference (1938), however, Poland did manage to get the Cieszyn (Teschen) territory it had been demanding in its dispute with Czechoslovakia. For a discussion of Polish foreign policy between the wars, see: Roman Debicki, *Foreign Policy of Poland, 1919–1939* (New York: Praeger, 1962).

[24]The fall of the Ukraine to the bolsheviks first dimmed the hopes for such a federation or alliance against the U.S.S.R., as the Ukraine was to have been a key member. Hope continued to fade as Poland became embroiled in major border disputes

ness of collective security through the League of Nations forced the Poles to rely on distant France (and later Britain) and on nonaggression treaties with the U.S.S.R. (1932) and with Germany (1934). There was considerable doubt in Poland about whether these arrangements could successfully provide security, but to the majority maintaining an independent course between its two neighbors seemed preferable to closer ties with either.

In matters of domestic policy most of the middle and upper classes—many intellectuals excepted—tended to support the status quo. To be sure, there was disagreement over specific issues, but there was no widespread support for any radical change in the socioeconomic system. The steps that had been and were being taken in the direction of social welfare, land reform, and economic development were generally considered sufficient. Although many people apparently felt that a greater degree of democracy would be desirable, they often had real doubts about whether such a political system would be practical for Poland in the light of its earlier experience with democracy.

The working-class belief system differed from the above primarily in that the workers were more radical in their demands for changing the status quo, wanted more freedom for the opposition, and were for the most part less interested in politics. Though there was a very significant democratic socialist movement within the working class, its strongest demands were

---

with Lithuania and Czechoslovakia, alienating not only these two states, but other potential members of the alliance as well. Even after tempers had cooled, however, it was clear that there was too much hostility, suspicion, and disagreement between the states involved to make a meaningful alliance possible.

13

for bread and butter objectives, and its leadership found it difficult to arouse much interest in radical, ideologically based reforms of the socioeconomic system. The Communist Party, illegal since 1919, had relatively few adherents. There were also a number of leftist splinter parties, but they were not strong politically.

The peasants were even more isolated from national politics. Their major links to the nation and state were through the church and (politically) through the relatively powerful Peasant (Piast) Party, which was strongly nationalistic and generally conservative except for its support for land reform. There was also a weaker, but more radical, left (Thurgutt) Peasant movement with most of its strength in the former Russian-occupied area of Poland.[25] Despite the activities of the leadership of the peasant political organizations, the bulk of the peasants had little interest in national politics and were oriented primarily toward their village and the church.

The Social System

The Political Subsystem.   After the Polish Republic was set up at the end of World War I, a democratic system of government was established with a relatively

[25]It is worth adding that among the Ukrainians of eastern Poland, and to a lesser extent the Belorussians, there was considerable anti-Polish nationalist sentiment. The Ukrainian nationalists' demands ranged from more cultural and political autonomy to union with the Ukraine. The communists, in fact, were able to exploit this nationalistic feeling to build a significant political movement in the Ukrainian territory of Poland. See R. V. Burks, *The Dynamics of Communism in Eastern Europe* (Princeton: Princeton U. Press, 1961).

weak executive. The general lack of unity in the newly reconstituted state produced an enormous number of political parties from which it was not possible to form a stable coalition. The governmental instability, lack of consensus, and the continual bickering among the parties made it impossible to reach agreement on a legislative program that could meet the needs of the nation or satisfy more than a minority of the politically active population.

In 1926 Marshal Pilsudski—supported by the army, the Socialist Party, and the communists—led a successful military coup. After gaining power, however, Pilsudski actively began to solicit support from the conservative elements in Poland who had opposed his rise to power, and he began to build an authoritarian regime. Pilsudski tried, unsuccessfully, to substitute a disciplined, broadly based national movement similar to that of Mussolini's Italy for what he and his close followers felt to be an ineffective experiment in democracy. The movement failed to achieve a broad base of support, however, because Pilsudski's concessions to the conservative industrialists, middle class, and land owners had alienated the center and the moderate left.[26]

The major effect of the coup was to reduce greatly the role of the legislative branch and to bring a stable, conservative government to power with Pilsudski directing activities from behind the scenes until his death. The Constitution of 1935, promulgated with-

[26]The center was represented by the right-wing Conservative Party, the powerful National Democratic Party, and so forth; the moderate left, by the Peasant (Piast) Party (SL) and the Polish Socialist Party (PPS) with its important labor union base.

out the degree of support of the Sejm (parliament) required under the 1921 Constitution, further strengthened the executive branch and the power of the government to control elections. Government action, an opposition boycott of the elections held under the new constitution, and popular disillusionment with the operation of parliamentary democracy in the pre-1926 period, resulted after 1935 in a virtual one-party legislature run by the government bloc (BBWR or The Nonparty Bloc for Co-operation with the Government—after 1937, the OZN or Camp of National Unity).

After Pilsudski's death, the country was ruled in more or less collective fashion by some of the dictator's political and military associates, who controlled both the executive branch and the government bloc in the Sejm. Like Pilsudski, they were primarily interested in preserving stability and the status quo, though they also promoted economic development and an expansion of Polish military strength. They were no more enthusiastic about democracy than Pilsudski had been and consequently put the most dangerous of the opposition in the concentration camp at Bereza.

Outside the government bloc the Polish Peasant Party (PSL)[27] and the Polish Socialist Party (PPS), both important centers of opposition, continued their respective activities of organizing agricultural consumers' and producers' co-operatives. The Communist Party of Poland (KPP), which had been illegal and

[27]After 1930 the Peasant (Piast) Party, which was strong in the former Austrian-occupied part of Poland, and the smaller, left-wing Thurgutt peasant movement, which was strong in former Russian-occupied Poland, merged to form the Polish Peasant Party (PSL).

effectively repressed since 1919, was numerically weak in the pre-entry period. It was dissolved completely in 1938 at Stalin's order, and most of its leadership was executed or imprisoned in the U.S.S.R. during the great purge.[28] There were also a number of left-wing splinter parties, but they were generally weak and poorly organized. The Roman Catholic Church, although potentially a powerful political force, supported the existing government as long as it did not attempt to weaken the Church's privileged position in Poland.

In the pre-entry period, then, no real democratic tradition had a chance to develop. Although there was in effect a one-party system during the latter part of the period, it was not a totalitarian system.[29]

As far as Poland's external relations were concerned, there was almost no integration between Poland and any other state in the pre-entry period aside from the normal diplomatic relations that any state is expected to have with other states. Poland did belong to the League of Nations, however, and took an active part in other international organizations, such as the ILO. As a sovereign state Poland theoretically could not be bound against its will, but its relatively weak

[28]For a history of the Polish Communist Party see: M. K. Dziewanowski, *The Communist Party of Poland* (Cambridge: Harvard U. Press, 1959).

[29]Pilsudski's government failed to develop any mass movement and did not change the basically pluralistic character of Polish society. The government and its bloc did not effectively penetrate the society. Its active base of support was primarily conservative interests, but it also depended on force and on public apathy and disillusionment with democracy to stay in power. There was relatively little police terror, however, and a great measure of personal freedom existed for all but the most active of the opposition.

power position did force the Poles to accept, reluctantly, the post-World War I boundary settlements with Germany and Czechoslovakia that were negotiated with the major powers.

Although there was virtually no formal institutional integration between Poland and other states, a good deal of substantive integration was achieved through normal diplomatic channels. In addition to the trade agreements discussed below, Poland negotiated an alliance with Rumania (1921), a treaty of consultation (1921) and military convention (1922) with France, and an agreement of mutual aid in the event of an armed attack with Great Britain (1939). In addition, nonaggression pacts were negotiated with the U.S.S.R. (1932) and with Germany (1934). It is worth noting that the most important substantive agreements were with France and Great Britain, states that were not then and are not now members of the communist system. The treaty with Rumania was designed primarily to protect Poland from being brought into the communist system by force. The nonaggression treaties provided only a very limited and passive sort of integration, and were negotiated only when it became clear that more effective security arrangements could not be worked out.

The Military Subsystem. Although military expenditures were high for peacetime, they were far from adequate to meet the needs of the Polish state, given its geographical situation, particularly after the rise of Hitler. It seems quite clear on the basis of its size alone—not to mention the objective results on the battlefield in 1939—that Poland was much weaker than either of its two powerful neighbors to the east and to the west, though considerably stronger than its other neighbors. Poland had a sizable and loyal army that was capable of fighting bravely, particularly in the defense of its own country. Its major weakness was that it was very poorly equipped with modern defensive weapons and had to bear the additional burden of a frontier with no natural line of defense against its major foes.

Poland, then, was far from self-sufficient in the area of security and military defense. Although the limited military integration that was achieved did not in any way compromise Polish independence, as Poland retained full control over its own diplomatic affairs and military forces, neither did it meet her needs, especially as 1939 approached and Poland's enemies grew relatively stronger and began to co-operate with one another.

The Economic Subsystem.[30] Though the government had instituted a rather extensive social welfare program right after World War I and had promoted economic development,[31] Poland remained a relatively poor state with an uneven distribution of wealth. A moderate land-reform program affecting about 2.7 million hectares had been carried out, but it was unsatisfactory to the smaller landholders and landless peasants. It also failed to solve the problem of small and scattered land holdings, despite the fact that the program also brought about the consolidation of

[30]For a general survey of Polish economic development through this period see: J. Taylor, *The Economic Development of Poland* (Ithaca: Cornell U. Press, 1952).

[31]For a study of interwar developments in the socioeconomic sphere see: Zweig, *Poland between Two Wars.*

about 5.4 million hectares of fragmented holdings. Only one-seventh of the farms were larger than 50 hectares (about 120 acres) in 1939. Most of the rest were small (under 12 acres), overpopulated, lacking in machinery, inadequately fertilized, and only moderately productive. Agricultural unemployment and rural poverty were widespread.

In large part because of the legacy of its experience under long foreign occupation, pre-entry Poland was one of the least industrialized states in Europe, with 60 per cent of its population dependent on agriculture and only 12.8 per cent dependent on industry and crafts in 1931.[32] There was considerable development of industry in the interwar period, however, and by 1939 the proportion of the population dependent on industry was probably closer to 20 per cent.

The economy was decidedly a mixed one. A significant part of Polish industry, most communications and transportation, and the banks were owned and controlled by the government. The state had a complete monopoly in the manufacture of salt, matches, alcohol, tobacco, and armaments. It owned the railroads and the airlines, 90 per cent of the merchant marine, 80 per cent of the chemical industry, and almost half the iron and metallurgical industry. The government also played an important role in capital accumulation, planning, and economic development. Its role in the development of the Central Industrial District (COP) in the previously nonindustrial heart

[32]*Rocznik Statystyczny, 1959,* p. 36. *Concise Statistical Yearbook of Poland, 1938,* p. 32, however, puts 19.4 per cent of the population in this category (on the basis of a broader definition of the category which excludes only those in agriculture, commerce, and communications).

of present-day Poland was particularly important. Private foreign capital also played a very significant role in the economic life of interwar Poland, especially in petroleum, public utilities, insurance, chemicals, and mining. In 1935 over 44 per cent of the capital of all Polish joint stock companies was foreign.[33]

During the period of occupation, Poland's major trading partners had been Germany, Austria, and Russia. Postwar political developments and the erection of customs barriers, however, altered this trade pattern, shifting much of Poland's trade to North America and the other countries of western Europe. Following the Polish-Soviet war (1920–21) friendly trade relations were eventually established with the U.S.S.R., but its trade with Poland was very limited throughout the interwar period. Trade with Germany, on the other hand, remained significant throughout this period, though its share of Poland's foreign trade declined from 26.9 per cent of imports and 34.3 per cent of exports in 1928 to 14.5 per cent of each in 1937,[34] in large part because of the tariff war that Germany waged against Poland between 1925 and 1934.

One interesting attempt at low-level regional economic integration was the so-called Agrarian Bloc Conference held in Warsaw in June, 1930, in an attempt to organize the states of the region in order to improve their economic bargaining position vis-à-vis the more industrialized states of western Europe. The conference was attended by delegates from Bulgaria,

[33]For a more detailed account of private foreign investment in Poland see: *Concise Statistical Yearbook of Poland, 1938,* pp. 98, 103–4.

[34]*Ibid.,* p. 157.

Czechoslovakia, Estonia, Hungary, Latvia, Poland, Rumania, and Yugoslavia. Luthuania was invited but did not attend. A permanent organization was created, and economic experts were to meet annually. It was active and reasonably successful for some years before the declining solidarity of the states involved made the organization decreasingly effective.[35]

In the economic realm then, except for the short-lived agrarian bloc organization and the international corporations operating in Poland, there was no formal institutional integration, though trade agreements were negotiated with a wide variety of states including Austria, Belgium, France, Switzerland, Turkey, the United Kingdom, Rumania, Yugoslavia, Germany, and the U.S.S.R. It is worth noting that the over-whelming bulk of the actual trade turnover was with states that were not then and are not now members of the communist system. In 1937 the U.S.S.R. accounted for only 1.2 per cent of Poland's imports and 0.4 per cent of its exports.[36] Of the present communist-ruled states only Czechoslovakia absorbed any significant percentage of Polish trade: in 1928, 6.3 per cent of imports and 11.8 per cent of exports; in 1937, 3.5 per cent of imports and 4.3 per cent of exports.[37] Germany was, indeed, an important trading partner, but judging from the nature of Poland's trade with its western neighbor—exports of foodstuffs and imports of industrial goods—much of this exchange must have been with that part of prewar Germany which is now part of Poland or the Federal Republic of Germany. By the end of the interwar period the United King-

---

[35]See Debicki, *Foreign Policy of Poland,* p. 66.
[36]*Concise Statistical Yearbook of Poland, 1938,* p. 157.
[37]*Ibid.*

dom was Poland's most important trading partner, followed closely by Germany and the United States. [Table No. 1 in the Appendix indicates the percentages of Polish imports and exports accounted for by Poland's most important trading partners in 1928 and in 1937, ranked according to their share of Polish trade in 1937.]

Poland was more self-sufficient economically than militarily, but its industry and economic development depended on the import of machinery and raw materials for the production of textiles and metals. Chemicals and pharmaceuticals, hides and leather products, machines and transport vehicles were also imported in significant quantities. Poland, however, was self-sufficient in all basic foodstuffs except fruits, fats and oils, and coffee, tea, and cocoa. Poland's primary exports were agricultural products, timber, coal, and textiles. Machinery and metal exports, however, were growing in importance. [Table No. 2 in the Appendix shows in some detail the states on which Poland was dependent for the import of its basic commodities. It is worth noting the degree of diversification in each category.]

Though Poland was dependent on the outside world for the import of many essential commodities, its trade was diversified enough so that in no major commodity area was it in any way completely dependent on any one state. Poland was dependent to a significant degree only on Great Britain, Germany, and the United States. It was not at all dependent on the present members of the communist system.

The Communications Subsystem. The interwar transportation and communications system was not highly developed and provided a major obstacle to internal trade and economic development. During the period of partition and occupation, Austria, Prussia, and Russia had built three separate transport and communications systems that integrated the three parts of Poland with their respective occupying powers, but not with each other. Although much improved, this situation had not been fully corrected by the end of the pre-entry period. Within Poland the transportation and communications network was also very uneven in density, most developed west of the Vistula River and in the Lvov area.

In addition to the isolation of many villages resulting from the sparse transportation and communications network, there were a number of other major barriers to the free flow of communications in Poland. The most important of these was the prejudice against the peasantry felt by the settled, middle-class urban dweller and the members of aristocracy. This bias was caused in part by the cultural gap between the classes and was reinforced by the peasants' lack of access to higher education. A second obstacle was the fairly rigid class structure, which isolated the workers from the middle and upper classes. A third barrier was the prejudice of the Polish population against the minority groups and the resentment of the latter toward the Poles. These obstacles were not insurmountable, but they certainly helped structure the flow of communications.

Although there was no formal integration with other states in this area (other than the normal international agreements), communications flowed freely across international boundaries to and from Poland. The bulk of the communications followed Poland's traditional cultural ties with western Europe and North America and its western-oriented tourist and trade patterns. Personal communications were especially heavy between Poland and those countries where there was a large Polish immigrant population (especially the United States).

The Socialization Subsystem. The school system, which was built up rapidly during the pre-entry period, was an important channel for teaching the dominant cultural values and nationalistic sentiments to the young people. Because of the very high dropout rate in elementary school—particularly in the villages—the Roman Catholic Church and the tradition-oriented peasant family were particularly important institutions in the socialization process. The Church also had some influence through religious education classes in the schools.

The general secondary schools, which accounted for about two-thirds of the pupils enrolled at that level in 1938, emphasized the humanities and sciences and were attended largely by the children of the middle class.[38] There was also a smaller, but growing, system of trade schools. Most primary school students were enrolled in state schools, but over one-third of the general secondary pupils and over one-half of the trade school pupils attended schools privately run.[39]

The schools of higher education were also dominated by the children of the middle and upper classes, though scholarships were available for qualified secondary school graduates.[40] Attendance at the schools of higher education followed roughly the class lines of the general secondary schools; there was, however, a

[38]*Ibid.,* p. 311 (for exact figures on the class origins of pupils and students).

[39]*Ibid.,* p. 309 (for exact figures).

[40]*Ibid.,* p. 328. In practice about 24 per cent of the students had some sort of scholarship in 1936–37.

higher drop-out rate at the end of secondary school for pupils of a working-class background.[41]

Radio, motion pictures, the press, and libraries played a more and more important role in socialization as these media increasingly penetrated the countryside and as the educational level gradually rose. The activities of the Peasant (Piast) Party and of the Polish Socialist Party were also very important in the political socialization of the peasants and workers because of the close association of these parties with the co-operative and union movements.

The Degree of Integration: Its Costs and Benefits

There were certainly no costs to Poland as a result of what little integration there was with other states, though there is some question about whether there were any benefits either, save the normal gains from foreign trade, travel, and cultural exchange. What little integration there was with the U.S.S.R.—namely, the 1932 nonaggression pact—may have raised some hopes for Polish security, but this was later proven to be without benefit after the secret Soviet–German agreements for the joint occupation of Poland were revealed. At the same time, however, Polish political and military co-operation with France, Rumania, and Great Britain was also demonstrated to be of questionable value in preventing invasion and conquest by either Germany or the U.S.S.R., though it may be argued that it prolonged the period of peace and independence. Nevertheless, Poland's allies were neither prepared nor in any position to send any substantial military supplies or personnel to aid in the defense of Poland or to protect its interests effectively in the dip-

[41]*Ibid.*, p. 311.

lomatic arena during or after the war. Despite these historical developments, it was widely believed at the time by the elite and general population that the alliance with France was beneficial and that any further integration with the U.S.S.R.—or with Germany— would prove to be much more costly.

There seems to have been widespread domestic support for the Polish government's policies on integration in the interwar period. Although there was some active support in Poland for more integration, there was no intense demand for it,[42] and after the early postwar years few people seriously called for extensive integration in the form of unified decision-making institutions. What demands there were for further integration called for closer economic, political, and military ties with the states lying between the U.S.S.R. and Germany and with the other states of northern and western Europe.[43] In this period neither the Polish ruling elite nor any significant group of the

[42]It is important to remember that integration would not have been without cost to the Poles, as the decision to integrate did not rest only with them. Closer ties with Czechoslovakia, for example, would have required not only giving up Polish claims to the disputed Cieszyn area, but also accepting the anti-Hungarian orientation of the Little Entente. Furthermore, Poland and Czechoslovakia did not see eye to eye on the issue of the relative danger of the U.S.S.R. and Germany, with Czechoslovakia (which had been spared an occupation by Russia) being more disposed toward cooperation with the U.S.S.R. See: P. S. Wandycz, *Czechoslovak-Polish Confederation and the Great Powers, 1940–1943,* Slavic and East European Series, vol. 3 (Bloomington: Indiana U. Publications, 1956), pp. 1–32.

[43]The major plans for integration were Pilsudski's post-World War I plan for a union of eastern European states and the later (1940–43) plan for a Confederation of Czechoslovakia and Poland. During the greater part of the interwar period, however, no plans were considered for such extensive integration. It was simply not considered possible.

population was asking for integration with the U.S.S.R., except possibly in the area of trade. The groups that did advocate closer integration with the U.S.S.R. were small and without much political power or influence and became fewer and weaker as the interwar period progressed. The ruling elite, of course, was particularly suspicious of collaboration with the Soviet Union.[44]

During the interwar period it proved impossible for Poland to work out closer political and military ties with the other states of central Europe because of their differing political orientations and perceived priorities, their mutual hostilities and suspicions, unwillingness to compromise on outstanding issues, and an inadequate sense of urgency. Even encouragement and urging from France and Britain did not succeed in overcoming these obstacles. After the initial years of the interwar period, only the most optimistic advocates of integration with the other states of central Europe had any expectation of any such change in the status quo in the near future. Though there was increasing apprehension about German demands and growing German and Soviet power, there seems to have been little expectation in Poland of anything like the drastic and involuntary changes in integration which were precipitated by World War II.

[44]The so-called Cracow group of historians, who had been advocating closer ties with one or the other of Poland's traditional enemies, had little important following in this period because of the general fear of bolshevism. A closer relationship with Germany also seemed out of the question with the rise of Hitler and his policies toward the East.

2: THE COMMUNIST TAKEOVER AND CONSOLIDATION OF POWER, 1939–48

The German invasion of Poland on September 1, 1939, and the Soviet move sixteen days later to occupy the eastern part of Poland began to lay the groundwork for Poland's entry into the communist party state system by initiating the destruction of the existing socioeconomic and political structures and forcing the Polish government into exile—first in Paris, then in London. The Soviet Union further contributed to this process between 1939 and 1941 by deporting to the interior of the Soviet Union approximately one and one-half million of the five million Poles under its occupation. It also executed somewhere between eight and sixteen thousand of the Polish officers who had surrendered to the Soviet forces in 1939.[1]

The Germans also unknowingly made their contribution to the consolidation of Soviet power. After their victory in 1939, large western segments of Poland were incorporated into the German Reich. The Germans deported about one and one-half million Poles from this territory to what remained of German-occupied central Poland (the so-called General Gov-

[1]See: J. K. Zawodny, *Death in the Forest: The Story of the Katyn Massacre* (Notre Dame: U. of Notre Dame Press, 1962).

ernment). Many government officials and community leaders were either executed or imprisoned in the early days of the occupation. Tens of thousands of other Poles were sent to German labor camps all over Europe during the war.[2]

In the course of the war over six million (22.2 per cent) of the twenty-seven million Poles and Jews living within the post-World War II boundaries died in military action, in concentration camps and work camps, or in on-the-spot executions—mostly at the hands of the Germans. The dead included virtually all the Polish Jews and a very high proportion of those with technical, administrative, and intellectual skills. Tens of thousands of others from this educated group fled the country in the course of the war and in the period immediately following. The net effect was the elimination of an important part of the politically active population, particularly those who would have been most openly opposed to Poland's transformation into a communist state and its integration into the communist system.[3]

[2]See: William F. Gingerich, *The German Administration of the General Government of Poland, 1939–1941* (Washington, D.C., 1949) and Poland, Gouvernment in Exile, Ministry of Information and Documentation, *The German Invasion of Poland* (London, 1940).

[3]For some accounts of wartime Poland see: Wladyslaw Anders, *An Army in Exile* (New York: Macmillan, 1949); Philip Friedman, *Martyrs and Fighters: The Epic of the Warsaw Ghetto* (New York: Praeger, 1954); Jan Karski, *Story of a Secret State* (Boston: Houghton Mifflin, 1943); Tadeusz Bor-Komorowski, *The Secret Army* (London: Gollancz, 1951); Stefan Korbonski, *Fighting Warsaw*, trans. F. B. Czarnomski (London: Allen and Unwin, 1956); Irene Oraka, *Silent Is the Vistula: The Story of the Warsaw Uprising*, trans. Marta Erdman (New York: Longmans Green, 1946); and Joseph Leib Tenenbaum, *Underground: The Story of a People* (New York: Philosophical Library, 1952).

Wartime physical damage and destruction were enormous, particularly in Warsaw and the industrial and port areas that Poland received from the Germans at the end of the war. The virtually complete destruction of Warsaw by the Germans after the failure of the Warsaw uprising of 1944 was of particular significance in aiding the communist take-over of Poland.[4] The demoralizing effect of the loss of the capital city and its historical buildings and monuments was important, but there were other effects as well. In the prewar period Warsaw had been the political and communications hub of a centralized political and economic system. In addition, the city was an important economic center in its own right. With Warsaw destroyed, the physical and psychological focal point of the old system was eliminated. In destroying Warsaw, which had been controlled by the Polish London government, the Germans also left the communists in

'Though the Germans were the ones who actually destroyed Warsaw, the consensus of the Western historians—and the Poles privately—is that the Soviet Union must also share the responsibility for three reasons: first, for its failure to send any more than token aid to help the uprising; second, by refusing to let American and British planes land on Soviet-occupied territory after dropping supplies; and third and most controversial, for delaying Soviet action against the Germans in the region of Warsaw until it was too late to prevent the destruction of the city and the German capture of the remnants of the anticommunist Home Army who had fought there virtually unaided for sixty-three days. The communists, on the other hand, argue that German military action and an overextended supply line made it impossible to take any decisive action earlier, and they blame the Polish London government and the Home Army for thinking primarily of their own political advantage and failing to co-ordinate their moves with those of the Soviet forces. Whatever the reasons for the Soviet failure to come to the aid of the Home Army in Warsaw, the German action made it easier for the Polish communist forces to gain control of Poland.

31

control of the only semblance of an organized center of national government in Poland: namely, the Committee of National Liberation, which had been organized earlier in the U.S.S.R., and the provisional government that it established.

It was the Soviet victory at the end of the war, however, that finally brought Poland under communist rule. As the Soviet armies pushed westward in 1944 and 1945, they supported the communist-dominated provisional government against the claims of the Polish government-in-exile in London and its supporters in Poland. After the Germans had been driven from Poland and the war brought to an end, the Soviet armies and the Soviet secret police continued to provide a protective shield for the new government while it was consolidating its own position. The absence of those who perished in the war at the hands of the Germans and Soviets and the great wartime destruction in Poland were of great help to the communists in their consolidation of power, as was the lack of willingness to intervene on the part of the Western allies.

Changes in the Environment

At the end of the war Poland was still surrounded on two sides by its old enemies, Germany and the U.S.S.R.; but for the moment, anyway, Germany lay in ruins under the occupation of the allied forces and was no immediate threat to Poland. On the other hand, the Soviet Union was considerably stronger than ever before and occupied a much more dominant position in central Europe. Moreover, the U.S.S.R. appeared determined to take advantage of its opportunity to transform the territory under its control into friendly socialist states.

In addition, Poland's former Baltic neighbors, Estonia, Latvia, and Lithuania, had been incorporated into the Soviet Union during the war. Rumania, Hungary, Bulgaria, Yugoslavia, and Soviet-occupied Germany had also been brought under communist rule. In 1948 Czechoslovakia was to meet the same fate, thus completely isolating Poland geographically from the noncommunist world except for its outlet to the sea.

The war also brought important boundary changes to Poland. The Soviet Union retained the area that it had occupied in 1939 (about one-third of Poland's former area), including the traditional cultural centers of Vilno and Lvov. In return, Poland received most of East Prussia, Gdansk (Danzig), and a sizable slice of territory from Germany proper as far east as the Oder and Neisse Rivers, including Wróclaw (Breslau) and Szczecin (Stettin). This territory in the north and west had once been part of Poland, but most of it had not been under Polish control since the fourteenth century. Technically, according to the agreements with the Western powers, the Poles were given these territories to administer until the signing of a peace treaty with Germany. As far as Poland and the U.S.S.R. were concerned, however, the territorial changes were final.[5]

The effect of these boundary changes was to push Poland roughly 130 miles to the west; to reduce its territory from 388.6 to 311.7 thousand square kilometers; to eliminate Latvia, Lithuania, and Rumania as

[5]There was also a general understanding by the western allies, however, that Poland was to receive these territories as compensation for its wartime losses at the hands of the Germans. See also: Edward J. Rozek, *Allied Wartime Diplomacy: A Pattern in Poland* (New York: Wiley, 1958).

neighbors; to reduce the length of its border from 5,529 to 3,538 kilometers; to increase the length of its coastline five times (to 694 kilometers), giving Poland the major ports of Gdansk and Szczecin and the smaller ports of Kolobrzeg (Kolberg), Darlowo (Rugenwalde), and Ustka (Stolpmünde); to increase the density of the rail and road network; to add the important Oder River to Poland's system of inland waterways; to give Poland all the damaged but important Silesian industrial basin, including extensive lignite deposits and significant coal, copper, and other mineral resources; to lose most of Poland's oil reserves in the southeast as well as the industry and good agricultural lands of the Lvov region; and to gain a smaller amount of good and traditionally well-managed agricultural land in the west.[6]

Despite the fact that the physical destruction wrought by the war had been great, most of the major damage to Poland's industrial and transport network had been repaired by the end of this period. The damage to housing, however, remained extensive, though most of the rubble had been cleared. Warsaw received a high priority in the reconstruction plans and was soon restored as the undisputed center of Polish culture and political power.

Demographic Changes

The war and the border changes also resulted in a net population loss to Poland of over 11.5 million people, including the estimated 6 million dead. During the early postwar period the population of the

[6]Poland actually lost a little over five million hectares of agricultural land, half of it cultivated (*Rocznik Statystyczny, 1959*, p. 170).

"recovered territories" (as the Poles call the once Polish land that they received from Germany at the end of the war) was very low since about 5 million of the Germans who had lived there left their homes with the retreating German armies and another 2.5 million who remained were deported to Germany after the war.[7] Despite the fact that the Polish government encouraged the 2,000,000 Poles displaced from the lost eastern provinces and the other Poles in overcrowded central Poland to move into the recovered territories, the population of these areas did not reach the prewar level until at least 1961.[8]

There was a significant rise in the birth rate after the war and an even greater increase in the rate of population growth, particularly in the recovered territories where the proportion of the population between ages 20 and 30 was close to 30 per cent. The percentage of Poles living in urban areas also increased during this period, owing both to the loss of the rural east and to the new emphasis on industrialization. This trend continued as postwar economic development progressed. The absolute number of the rural population remained about the same, however.

One politically significant result of the war and the great shifts in population was that Poland for the first time in 500 years had an ethnically and religiously homogeneous population. Over 98 per cent of the people were Polish, and 95 per cent were Catholic. Of

[7] This left about 1.5 million Poles and Polish-German families. See also: H. Zielinski, *Population Changes in Poland, 1939–1950*, Mid-European Studies Center Publication, no. 16 (New York, 1954).

[8] In 1961 the Poles announced a population of 7.8 million for the recovered territories. Zachodnia Agencja Prasowa, *Polskie Ziemie Zachodnie i Polnocne* (Poznan, 1961), p. 83.

the 3.5 million Jews in prewar Poland, only 100,000 or so remained.[9] Many thousands who had managed to escape the German gas chambers or who had spent the war in the U.S.S.R. emigrated to Israel at the first opportunity. In spite of the Polish acquisition of so much German-populated territory, and because of the mass emigrations and deportations, there were only about 150,000–200,000 people who considered themselves Germans remaining in Poland by the end of this period.[10] There were many thousands more, of course, who had at least some German ethnic background. After the loss of the eastern provinces there were only about 300,000 Belorussians and 100,000 Ukrainians still in Poland. There were also a scattering of other minority groups, including perhaps 25,000–35,000 gypsies.

Changes in the Belief System

The death and emigration of so many of those of the Polish middle and upper classes and the extensive

[9]The Jewish population of Poland from 1944–56 varied considerably because of the Jewish emigration from the U.S.S.R. to Poland and the subsequent emigration from Poland to Israel. Exact figures therefore are difficult to obtain.

[10]See also: Thedor Scheider, ed., *The Expulsion of the German Population from the Territories East of the Oder-Neisse Line* (Bonn, n.d.); W. M. Drzewieniecki, *The German-Polish Frontier* (Chicago: Polish Western Association of America, 1959); Zbigniew Jordan, *The Oder-Neisse Line* (London: Polish Freedom Movement, 1952); Jozef Kokot, *The Logic of the Oder-Neisse Frontier* (Poznan: Wydawnictwo Zachodnie, 1959); Leszek Kosinski, "Demographic Problems of the Polish Western and Northern Territories," *Geographical Essays on Eastern Europe* ed. Norman J. G. Pounds, Russian and East Europe Series, vol. 24 (Bloomington: Indiana U. Publications, 1961), pp. 28–53; and Wolfgang Wagner, *The Genesis of the Oder-Neisse Line: A Study in the Diplomatic Negotiations during World War II* (Stuttgart: Bretano-Verlag, 1957).

wartime destruction and postwar social upheaval considerably altered the dominant values in Poland. The old aristocratic and middle-class culture was by no means destroyed since it had greatly penetrated all Polish thinking. It was nevertheless true that the effects of the war and communist rule had made working-class values, a belief in the need for social cooperation and centralized planning, support for the nationalization of industry, land reform, more extensive social welfare programs, and at least a grudging appreciation for the Soviet Union much more prevalent than before the war. Most of the old dominant belief system remained, however, including the strong nationalism and individualism, the identification of the church with the state, and the Western cultural orientation. The faith of the Poles in the West, though, had been badly shaken as it became clear that Poland could not depend on distant allies to defend it from its enemies, east or west. There was also considerable disenchantment over the lack of support for Polish interests displayed by the Western allies in the course of the war and the political settlements that followed.

Despite the good will generated for the U.S.S.R. by the Red Army in its liberation of Poland, the net effect of Soviet activities during and immediately after the war was the reinforcing and in some ways the strengthening of the Poles' negative attitude toward its eastern neighbor. The Soviet occupation of eastern Poland in 1939 and its permanent annexation after the war, the deportation of one and one-half million Poles to the U.S.S.R. between 1939 and 1941, the Katyn massacre of Polish officers,[11] the failure of the Soviet Union to help the Poles during the Warsaw Uprising, the behavior of Soviet troops in Poland,

[11]See: Zawodny, *Death in the Forest.*

37

Soviet looting operations, Soviet support for an unwanted communist government, and the activities of the Soviet secret police, all contributed to this Polish attitude.

In addition to the obvious goal of rebuilding the country, a primary goal for most Poles was to get Soviet troops out of Poland and to remove the communists from power. If this was not the most important goal for the majority of the Poles, it was shared at least to some degree by an overwhelming proportion of the people. As the communists consolidated their power and the Poles saw that the Western allies were not willing or able to do anything about it, however, it became increasingly clear that Poland would unavoidably be dominated by the U.S.S.R. and ruled by the Polish communists and their supporters. The fact that the strongest, most uncompromising, best organized, and most able opposition to the communists had either been killed in the war, imprisoned by the communists, or had fled the country also reduced the priority of this goal compared to what it might have been otherwise. In addition, most Poles were tired of war and fighting and felt that the moderate program of the coalition government offered more hope than did active resistance.

In short, the effects of the war when combined with the political skills of the communists, the backing of the Polish Soviet secret police, and the threat of open military intervention enabled the new ruling elite to neutralize the opposition and unite the nation around the new task of rebuilding Poland and getting the country moving again. This was something all Poles agreed had to be done, and the great majority of the people had no serious objections to the basic economic means by which the communists proposed to mobilize

Poland for this purpose. The workers and peasants, for example, had no strong ideological objections to the nationalization of the basic means of production. Moreover, a great many factory owners and managers were dead or had fled the country. Consequently the communists had little difficulty in convincing most people that the only way to get the economy moving again was through nationalization.

Another very important Polish postwar objective was the holding and development of the recovered territories. Perhaps no other single issue united the Polish people more. The importance of the recovered territories was emphasized by the loss of the land in the east to the U.S.S.R. and the widespread belief that it was lost forever. This feeling about the recovered territories grew as more and more Poles moved into the new territory and as increasingly large investments were made to rebuild and expand industry there.

The majority of the peasants had no objection to land reform, but nearly all of them felt very strongly about maintaining ownership and control over their individual plots of land and consequently were very much opposed to collectivization in any form—at least for themselves.

The small minority of communists, however, had a different structure of values and goals. Though many of the nominal members and supporters may not have agreed—especially those who joined after the Red Army moved into Poland—for the hard core of the Polish Workers' Party the major goal was the consolidation and maintenance of their power and the transformation of Poland into a socialist state with the communists in charge. It is important to remember, though, that probably a majority of the Polish communists—even many of those in the hard core—were at the same time Polish nationalists and shared in the prewar middle-class culture. This became increasingly so as the PPR made a serious effort to build its membership from the 20,000 adherents it had in mid-1944 (see Chap. II, n. 42). Although the PPR members may have wanted to see a socialist Poland, few of them wanted to see it ruled by the CPSU or exploited economically by the U.S.S.R. Memories of the fate of the prewar Polish Communist Party undoubtedly reinforced this feeling. Moreover, a good many Polish communist leaders, including Gomulka, did not believe that Poland should automatically adopt all the Soviet institutions or methods of building socialism.[12]

At the same time, most of the communist leaders must have seen that they could not have come to power without the help of the U.S.S.R. and that for some time at least their positions would depend on the Soviet presence to protect them from Western intervention and popular unrest at home. The U.S.S.R. therefore had another powerful lever to insure that the Polish leadership would not ignore its wishes.

In addition, there was within the PPR a group of communists who could be expected to follow the orthodox Moscow party line not only out of practical necessity but also because they believed in it religiously. Most of this group worked at lower and middle levels in the Party and were often politically naive in their faith. Because of the Soviet influence when the PPR and the new government were set up there were also others in key positions or power, many of

---

[12]See, for example, Gomulka's speeches, particularly those touching on agriculture, in: *W Walce o Democracje Ludowa* (Warsaw, 1947).

them trained in the Soviet Union, who out of some combination of faith, opportunism, and necessity were willing to follow Moscow's lead on virtually all issues. For the moment, however, owing to the small number of able, orthodox Polish communists available to fill the needs of consolidation of power, the U.S.S.R. also allowed some of the more unorthodox and nationalist-oriented Polish communists, such as Gomulka, to share the leadership.

The changes brought about by the war and the communist take-over certainly increased the similarity between Polish culture and the culture of the U.S.S.R. and the other system members, but on the whole the gap between them remained nearly as wide as before (particularly in relation to the Soviet Union), despite the efforts to spread communist beliefs in Poland.

The formal structure of Polish society, however, began to acquire an increasing resemblance to that of the U.S.S.R. as almost all institutions were patterned after the Soviet model. This was particularly true of government and economic institutions. These outward similarities, however, could not really disguise the underlying differences in tradition, language, religion, and ethnic background and were insufficient to provide a basis for building a sense of common identity or community with the U.S.S.R. and the rest of the communist world. In addition, the position of the church, the continued existence of private enterprise, noncollectivization of agriculture, and the presence of a host of front organizations and political parties distinguished Polish from Soviet society. (Most of these differentiating characteristics present in Poland, however, were also present in the other "people's democracies.")

Changes in the Social System

The Political Subsystem.[13] During the wartime occupation, a Polish government-in-exile had been set up in London. It directed an extensive underground movement during the war, competing with a much smaller communist underground movement that was organized after the German invasion of the Soviet Union.

In the course of the war the Soviet Union revived the Communist Party of Poland under the name of the Polish Workers' Party (PPR). It dominated the Soviet-sponsored National Council of the Homeland (KRN) and its executive body, the Polish Committee of National Liberation (PKWN), which by drawing members of other political parties and organizations into its membership attempted to provide a facade of respectability for the establishment of a communist-controlled government in Poland. The KRN officially proclaimed itself the sole source of authority in Poland on July 22, 1944, after Soviet forces had pushed beyond the present boundaries of Poland, and a provisional government was officially established in Warsaw on December 31.[14] It was recognized by the U.S.S.R. in early January, 1945. At Yalta the Western allies insisted that the base of the new government be broadened to include more noncommunist leaders.[15]

[13]See also: Z. Brzezinski, *The Soviet Bloc* (New York: Praeger, 1961) for the best over-all account of developments in Poland in relation to the communist system from 1944 to 1960.

[14]For a list of members and party affiliations see: Marian Malinowski, ed., *Polska Partia Robotnicza, Kronika,* Jan., 1942–May, 1945 (Warsaw: Wiedza Powszechna, 1962) p. 273.

[15]There were noncommunists in the group, too, however, such as Osobka Morawski, the PKWN Chairman, Andrzej Witos, Rola Zymierski, and others willing to co-operate with the communists.

A broader-based Polish Provisional Government of National Unity was finally formed in July, 1945, but the Polish communist elite still clearly maintained control.[16] The Polish elite was dependent on the U.S.S.R. for direct and indirect help in keeping it in power, though this dependence decreased somewhat as the communist consolidation of power continued. Even by the end of 1948, however, it is very doubtful that the elite could have remained in power without the ultimate threat of Soviet intervention.

The major link that allowed the Soviet Union to control Polish affairs was the Polish Workers' Party, whose leaders not only shared many ideological objectives with the Soviet leaders, but were also dependent on them for their position and power in Poland and were always in danger of being replaced if the U.S.S.R. were less than satisfied with their performance. This constant threat was made effective by the information-gathering system provided by the Soviet secret police, the Soviet Embassy, and the Soviet personnel in the Polish government, Party, and other Polish organizations. Despite this extensive and effective network of Soviet control over Poland, in practice the Polish communists still made most of the actual

[16]For some accounts of the communist victory in Poland see: Jan Ciechanowski, *Defeat in Victory* (Garden City: Doubleday, 1947); Stefan Korbonski, *Warsaw in Chains,* trans. Norbert Guterman (New York: Macmillan, 1959); Arthur Bliss Lane, *I Saw Poland Betrayed* (New York: Bobbs-Merrill, 1948); Stanislaw Mikolajczyk, *The Pattern of Soviet Domination* (London: S. Low, Marston, 1948); Czeslaw Milosz, *The Seizure of Power,* trans. Celina Wienewska (New York: Criterion Books, 1955); E. J. Rozek, *Allied Wartime Diplomacy* (New York: Wiley, 1958); and Anna L. Strong, *I Saw the New Poland* (Boston: Little, Brown, 1946). The book by Strong is strongly biased in favor of the Polish communists but nevertheless provides an interesting contrast to the accounts that are written from the opposite point of view.

decisions, though within the limits set by the U.S.S.R. The common goals shared by the PPR and the CPSU leaders in this period and the indirect threat of intervention made detailed control by the CPSU unnecessary. Both the active operations of the Soviet secret police and the more passive threat of the Red Army helped immeasurably in the neutralization of the anticommunist elements in Poland and in convincing the people to view the new government as inevitable and, therefore, deserving of support in its organization of the nation for reconstruction.

Outside the government the Polish communists and their supporters waged a war against the opposition with the assistance of the Soviet secret police and supported by the presence of the Red Army. The remaining members of the noncommunist underground, actual or potential political opposition leaders who refused to co-operate with the government, former (German) nazis, and those who collaborated with the German authorities were the main targets.[17]

One further important integrating link in this period was Poland's long-range dependence on the U.S.S.R. for the retention of its recovered territories. Though this dependence was not yet widely perceived

[17]The communists made effective use of the supporters they had been able to recruit from the left wings of the Polish Socialist Party (PPS) and the Peasant Party (PSL). After the war the left wing of the PPS had managed to take over the party and maintain control and was very useful in helping the communists infiltrate the trade unions and the co-operative movement. The left wing of the PSL was also useful in helping the communists gain control of the countryside through the organization of the Peasant Self-Help Union, which was officially established in late 1944 to aid in the implementation of the land reform program. The left wing of the PSL also helped set up separate peasant parties to rival the PSL proper, headed by Mikolajczyk and supporting the London government's point of view.

by the general population, the communists were quick to exploit it by doing everything possible to keep alive memories of the war and the fear of a rearmed Germany in the future.

Inside the formal institutions of government the communists and their supporters tried to ease out Mikolajczyk and the other more unco-operative members of the coalition. The electoral machinery and procedures in the election of 1947 were arranged to the advantage of the communists and the rest of the government bloc—the Polish Workers' Party (PPR), the Polish Socialist Party (PPS), the Peasant Party (SL), and the Democratic Party (SD). In addition, intimidation, interference, and special administrative obstacles were put in the way of the other parties, particularly in the case of the powerful Polish Peasant Party (PSL).

Until 1948, however, the communists, while playing a leading role in the government, publicly emphasized the coalition nature of the government and tried to win the confidence of the population with a moderate platform that promised something for nearly everyone: for the workers—to get the factories running again and to end unemployment; for the peasants—a land reform program (begun in 1944) and no collectivization; for both the workers and peasants—educational opportunities for their children and new prestige; for the small entrepreneurs—a three-sector economy with a place for private enterprise; for the nationalists—the rebuilding of Warsaw and the defense of the recovered territories; for the religious—reconstruction of the church buildings and freedom to worship.[18]

[18]See, for example, the speeches of Wladyslaw Gomulka, *W Walce o Democracje Ludowa* (Warsaw, 1947).

For the moment the Polish Workers' Party was too weak to hold power by itself—even with the help of the Polish and Soviet secret police and the threat of the Red Army. The communists had to depend not only on the passive support or indifference of most of the population, but also on the technical and administrative skills of noncommunists in important positions until they could win enough followers and train their own men to occupy all the key positions. The need for men with administrative and technical skills was one of the reasons for the merger of the PPR and the PPS in December, 1948, to form the Polish United Workers' Party (PZPR).

Despite official adherence to a parliamentary form of government, the Polish Workers' Party in practice controlled all the formal institutions of government and provided both the initiative for and the check on their operations. Behind the Party stood the U.S.S.R. and the CPSU, which operated through the Soviet Embassy in Warsaw, the Soviet secret police, the Red Army, and the Soviet citizens and agents who served as advisors or who held positions in the Polish government and in other Polish institutions.

Political parties in this period served at best as channels through which the interests of their supporters could be brought to the attention of the communists and negotiated with them. The more the political parties were infiltrated by the communists and their supporters, however, the more they began to serve primarily as instruments of political education and control over the masses rather than as channels of interest articulation.

As before the war, the most powerful single group outside the government was the Roman Catholic church. The church remained largely neutral in politics, however, and was willing to support the government on any issue it felt to be in the interest of the Polish people and the Polish state. Though it did not openly oppose the communists, there was no secret about the fact that the church adamantly disapproved of them and their ultimate objectives.[19] During this period the two most important active opposition groups—the Polish Peasant Party and the noncommunist underground—were virtually eliminated as an organized opposition.[20] Many other social groups were weakened or brought under communist control during this period by infiltration, as in the case of the trade unions, scouts, and Red Cross. New mass front organizations were also set up in this period to increase the government's ability to control the population and to weaken and woo away the membership of established organizations. Examples of such front organizations include the League of Soldiers' Friends, the League of Women, the Polish-Soviet Friendship Society, peace committees, and youth organizations.

Polish relations with the other Communist-ruled states were formalized in a series of Treaties of Friendship, Collaboration, and Mutual Assistance. The first was signed with the U.S.S.R. (April 21, 1945) and was followed by a similar treaty with Yugoslavia (March 18, 1946)—denounced September 29, 1949—and Czechoslovakia (March 10, 1947). Later, similar treaties were also made with Bulgaria (May 29, 1948), Hungary (June 18, 1948), and Rumania (January 26, 1949). A Treaty of Friendship with the

[19]See also: Vladimir Gsovski, ed., *Church and State behind the Iron Curtain* (New York: Praeger, 1955).

[20]See: Korbonski, *Warsaw in Chains* and Mikolajczyk, *The Pattern of Soviet Domination*.

G.D.R. (June 6, 1950) completed the series.[21] The bilateral Treaties of Friendship, Collaboration, and Mutual Assistance created defense alliances between the given states, prohibiting them from entering into coalitions with states opposing the interests of the cosignatories and requiring them both to help protect the peace and oppose any aggressive action from a re-armed Germany or its allies. They also emphasized the sovereignty of the parties to the treaty, noninterference in domestic affairs, and equality in their relations. The treaties also called for future economic and cultural co-operation.[22]

There was no political integration with the West aside from the normal diplomatic relations that the Polish government carried on after it had been recognized by the major powers of the world. Poland also took an active part in the U.N. and other international organizations, however, though its position always closely followed that of the U.S.S.R.[23]

[21]Note the exclusion of Albania.

[22]See also *Zagadnienia Prawne Konstytucji Polskiej Rzeczpospolitej Ludowej,* (Warsaw, 1954), III, 540–99; and Z. Brzezinski, *The Soviet Bloc,* pp. 108–11.

[23]Throughout this period, Poland, Czechoslovakia, and Yugoslavia were the only eastern European communist-ruled states in the U.N. (Hungary, Rumania, Bulgaria, and Albania were not admitted to membership until 1955, though they took part in many of the specialized agencies.) Poland was particularly active in the U.N. Economic Commission for Europe and in the specialized agencies of the U.N., participating more than any other communist-ruled state except Yugoslavia. Poland did not participate in the Intergovernmental Maritime Consultative Organization, the World Bank, IMF, or FAO; Poland joined the communist boycott of the ILO; in 1950 followed the earlier Soviet withdrawal from the WHO; and joined the rest of the communist bloc in its boycott of all U.N. agencies except the ICJ.

The Military Subsystem. Though exact figures are difficult to obtain, in general the Polish armed forces were small and poorly equipped following the demobilization after World War II. Many of the officers and men from the Polish army that had been fighting in the west did not return to Poland. Much of the postwar Polish army had been recruited from among the Polish deportees of 1939–41 and had fought with the Red Army on the eastern front. Others had been conscripted from the Polish population as the Red Armies pushed westward across Poland. During the war the line officers of the Polish units were almost entirely Russian.[24] After the war some of the officers returning from the west were admitted to the armed

[24]The Political-educational officer, however, was in most cases a Pole—no doubt in part, at least, to facilitate the problem of communication, which was particularly complicated in this post—or at least someone of Polish descent. See Ignacy Blum, *Z Dziejow Aparatu Politycznego Wojska Polskiego* (Warsaw, Wydawnictwo Ministerstwa Obrony Narodowej, 1957), p. 15. See also: *Z. Dziejow Wojska Polskiego w Latach,* 1945–1948 (Warsaw, MON, 1960).

It is also worth noting at this point that the distinction between a Pole and a Russian or Soviet was often fuzzy since many of the officers—as well as economic advisors, technicians, members of the secret police, and so forth—were, indeed, Poles by birth or ancestry but had often lived for much or all of their lives in the U.S.S.R., a factor that contributed heavily to their political views and loyalties. Cases were not unknown where the "Pole" spoke practically no Polish. On the other hand, the Soviet officers were also permitted to accept Polish citizenship by a decree of the Supreme Soviet [*Vedomosti Verkhovnogo Soveta,* no. 35 (June 30, 1944)]. Accepting Polish citizenship and accepting positions in the Polish armed forces also affected their outlook and loyalties over time. Although the incidents are not documented, the Poles sometimes tell of cases where Soviet officers in the Polish armed forces openly sided with the Poles in disputes with the U.S.S.R., particularly during the October, 1956, political crisis.

forces as officers. Others were increasingly recruited from among the worker and peasant classes.

In the military sphere Soviet control was much more direct than in politics, with effective control lying in the hands of Soviet officers and advisors who received their orders directly from Soviet sources rather than through Polish channels. Both during and after the war the top Polish military leadership was carefully screened by the U.S.S.R. before being appointed. Soviet military advisors and officers exercised considerable authority in the Polish armed forces if they did not in fact have full control.

In addition to the armed forces proper and the secret police, an Internal Security Corps and a Citizens' Militia were formed. The Polish secret police worked closely with the Soviet secret police, which exercised a very large measure of control over its Polish counterpart.

The Economic Subsystem. In September, 1944, the Soviet-sponsored provisional government issued a land reform decree affecting almost 9.8 million hectares (three million hectares of it within the prewar boundaries).[25] Farms with over 100 hectares (247 acres), those with 50 hectares of arable land, and land owned by Germans or German collaborators was to be expropriated. This land was to be redistributed to the landless peasants and to those displaced from the former Polish territory in the east. About 60 per cent of the expropriated land was distributed in this way, but the government retained full control over the rest and used much of it to set up state farms.[26] Otherwise,

[25]*Dziennik Ustaw,* no. 3 (Jan. 19, 1945).

[26]For figures (based on official Polish sources) regarding the amount of land expropriated and distributed as of 1948, see: *Foreign Agriculture,* nos. 7–8 (1953), pp. 140–42.

agricultural land remained almost entirely in private hands during this period, and the Party emphasized that there were no plans for collectivization.

Early in 1946 an extensive nationalization law was promulgated, giving the government control of all major economic institutions and in theory providing compensation to the former owners in the form of state bonds.[27] This nationalization also virtually eliminated foreign investment in Poland and gave the government almost complete control over the economy.

The first postwar years were spent largely in reconstruction and getting the economy back into operation, a considerable task in light of the great destruction in the industrial areas. Poland received nearly half a billion dollars in UNRRA aid in this period,[28] about 70 per cent of it coming from the United States. In addition between 1946 and 1949 Poland received another 675 million dollars in grants, loans, and credits from other states and international organizations (mostly from the U.S.S.R., but including 90 million dollars from the U.S.).[29] A 1947 loan request to the IBRD for 600 million dollars, however, was refused. In the same year the Poles first expressed real interest in participating in the Marshall Plan but then—presumably in response to Soviet pressure—refused to

[27]*Dziennik Ustaw,* no. 3 (Feb. 5, 1946).

[28]UNRRA, *Report of the Director General to the Council for the Period July 1, 1947 to December 31, 1947* (Washington, D.C., 1948), p. 204. For more recent figures see U.S. International Co-operation Administration, *U.S. Foreign Assistance and Assistance from International Organizations (July 1, 1945 through June 30, 1960),* p. 18. Of the $2.9 billion in relief supplies provided by UNRRA, Poland received 16 per cent, more than any other state except China (18 per cent). For more details see: George Woodbridge, ed., UNRRA, vol. 3 (New York: Columbia U. Press, 1950), p. 428.

[29]Halecki, *Poland,* p. 455.

take part and became active critics of the U.S. aid plan. Reconstruction was further complicated by organized Soviet looting operations aimed at removing everything of economic value in the recovered territories.[30] Before the Poles could persuade the Soviet Union to stop this operation, the latter had managed to take perhaps half a billion dollars worth of goods and equipment.

After the war foreign trade became a state monopoly. In the immediate postwar period trade turnover was generally considerably below the prewar level, though it increased rapidly and surpassed the 1938 level by the end of this period. There was generally a drop in exports (with the exception of coal) and an increase in imports as a result of the war and the needs of reconstruction. There was a particularly sharp rise in the import of foodstuffs, chemicals, petroleum, machinery, and transport vehicles and a drop in the import of most consumer goods (except for UNRRA food, clothing, and medicine).[31]

Economically, Poland was considerably less self-sufficient than in the pre-entry period because of the problem of reconstruction brought about by the war, the loss of its oil resources to the U.S.S.R., the net loss of agricultural land in the boundary shift, and the death, emigration, and political unacceptability of so many skilled and able Poles. Polish dependence on food imports was further increased by wartime damage to agricultural lands, the shortage of fertilizer, and general neglect. As new industries were established,

[30]There was also some of this type of looting reported in the prewar Polish territory, but it was not as extensive. The U.S.S.R. justified the looting of the former German territories as a part of the compensation due the Soviet Union from Germany.

[31]Glowny Urzad Statystyczny, *Rocznik Statystyczny, 1949* (Warsaw, 1950), pp. 104–5.

dependence on the outside for additional raw materials and markets steadily grew. This increased economic dependence on other states had important consequences for Poland's integration into the communist world.

Immediately after the war there was a marked shift in the direction of Polish trade. Except for UNRRA shipments (most of which came from the United States), the bulk of Poland's trade was with the U.S.S.R. and the other communist-ruled states. Within the communist world the U.S.S.R., East Germany, and Czechoslovakia were Poland's most important trading partners. Although there was a sharp initial decline in the communist system's share of Polish trade from a high of over 90 per cent in 1945 to a low of 31 per cent in 1947, reflecting the size of the UNRRA shipments, thereafter the proportion of trade with other communist-ruled states began to rise rapidly as both the U.S.S.R. and the West (particularly the United States) began to put restrictions on Polish trade with the noncommunist world.[32]

Though good statistics and reliable evidence are scarce in most cases, there is good reason to believe that even in this early postwar period the Poles were forced to make unfavorable trade agreements at discriminatory prices with the U.S.S.R.[33] The most

[32]The United States, for example, rescinded Poland's most favored nation status and discouraged the export of strategic goods from the West to the member states of the communist system.

[33]See, for example, Halecki, *Poland,* p. 463, and his example of the difference in price between Polish sugar exported to the U.S.S.R. and Czech sugar imported to Poland. See also: M. Dewar, *Soviet Trade with Eastern Europe, 1945–1949* (London: Royal Institute of International Affairs, 1951); and Alfred Zauberman, *Economic Imperialism: The Lesson of Eastern Europe* (London: Ampersand, Ltd., Bellman Books, 1955).

notable example of such discriminatory agreements was the coal agreement of August 16, 1945, which obligated Poland to deliver large quantities of coal to the U.S.S.R. at a price about 8–9 per cent of that which Poland could have earned by selling it in the West where coal was in short supply.[34]

Poland also apparently paid most of the expense of the maintenance of Soviet troops on Polish soil; and there is no evidence that the U.S.S.R. ever compensated Poland in more than token fashion for its extensive services in providing rail and road facilities for Soviet transports to and from East Germany.

In addition, at the Potsdam Conference the U.S.S.R. promised to assign to Poland 15 per cent of all war reparations collected from Germany. There is no evidence that Poland ever received more than a fraction of what had been promised.[35] The U.S.S.R. did, however, offer some credits to Poland in the postwar period. The credits promised (March 5, 1947 and January 26, 1948) amounted to about two billion rubles (or, at the official rate, almost half a billion dollars).[36]

The most useful Soviet aid was the 28.85 million

[34]Though the amount of the special coal deliveries was reduced in 1947, the cost to Poland in lost foreign exchange earnings in the West probably amounted to at least half a billion dollars by the time these special deliveries ended in 1956. See also: S. J. Zyniewski, "Coal in Poland's Economy and Foreign Trade," *Journal of Central European Affairs,* 19 (1959).

[35]Poland probably received at the most 1 to 2 per cent of the reparations collected by the U.S.S.R.

[36]It seems likely that this figure considerably inflates the actual value of the credits, owing to the prices set by the U.S.S.R. and the quality of the goods received compared to what could have been purchased in the West with the same amount of hard currency. There is also some reason to believe that the

dollar gold loan included in the March 5, 1947, Agreement on Technical Co-operation and Economic and Military Assistance to Poland. The Soviet Union also provided a large number of blueprints and technical advisors who (in addition to helping to keep Poland under Soviet control) made a significant contribution to the process of reconstruction and economic development, though they were particularly concentrated in areas of development which would be most useful in supplying Soviet needs. Moreover, these advisors and technicians were not provided by the U.S.S.R. without cost to Poland.

One other important development in this period was the series of technical assistance treaties which the U.S.S.R. began to sign with the Communist-ruled states of eastern Europe, beginning with Poland and Czechoslovakia in 1947. These treaties provided for an exchange of technical documentation without cost, except for a nominal charge for reproduction. This availability of low-cost documentation proved to be of great assistance to the Polish economy during the following period of economic development.[37] In July,

---

amount actually delivered fell considerably short of the plan. Finally, it is unclear what relationship this aid had to reparations payments from Germany—for example, whether it was intended as part of the reparations due Poland or was to be compensation for the industrial goods taken from the former German areas of Poland.

[37]See: Michael Kaser, *COMECON: Integration Problems of the Planned Economies* (London: Oxford U. Press, 1965), pp. 42–43. The network of technical collaboration treaties linking each of the East European states with the others was not completed until mid-1955, though the U.S.S.R. had earlier signed similar treaties with Bulgaria (1950), Hungary (1950), the G.D.R. (1951), and Albania (1952), following a recommendation of the Second Session of the Council of Mutual Economic Assistance in 1949.

1947, Poland and Czechoslovakia signed an important economic co-operation agreement that envisioned a wide range of potential co-operative endeavor and an eventual economic union.[38]

Nevertheless, Poland was not yet fully integrated economically with the communist system or with the U.S.S.R., despite the increase in the percentage of trade with the communist-ruled states compared with the pre-entry period. Not only was a sizable percentage of Polish trade with the West (except in 1946), but the goods that were most important to Poland for reconstruction and economic development were also to be found primarily outside the communist world. Though Poland had materials that were needed by the other communist-ruled states for their own reconstruction and development—most notably coal—the food and machinery that Poland needed most were in short supply there. The UNRRA aid and the other grants, loans, and credits that Poland received from the West were undoubtedly considerably more important than the aid which Poland received from the U.S.S.R. in this period, particularly if one considers the quality of the goods and subtracts Poland's losses to the U.S.S.R. in unpaid German reparations and lost coal earnings. Nevertheless, there was certainly more integration with the com-

[38]In 1949, however, the Soviet Union forced the cancellation of all the provisions of the treaty except those for the exchange of technical information—following the new emphasis on autarchy, the campaign against national deviation, and the attempt to increase Soviet control over eastern Europe by minimizing the amount of contact between the government and Party officials of the individual eastern European states. Note that the Bulgarian-Yugoslav treaty of 1947, incorporating Dimitrov's project for a Balkan federation, also met the same fate.

munist system than in the pre-entry period.[39] The mechanism by which this integration was achieved, as with political integration, was an informal one, using both the traditional channels of diplomacy and trade delegations and the newer methods of Soviet influence and control.[40]

The Communications Subsystem. Though much of the physical communications and transport network was destroyed during the war, it was replaced very rapidly. Because of the addition of the former German territory with its good communications and transportation facilities and the loss of the less well-served eastern areas, Poland soon had a denser network than before the war. Communications within the country became more centralized as well, with many communications moving out from Warsaw through Party and government channels. There was also increasing penetration of the countryside to reach formerly isolated individuals as the period progressed. With the nationalization of the major economic enterprises and

[39]The Polish coal shipments to the U.S.S.R. and the other trade agreements that Poland was beginning to make with the members of the system, of course, must be considered part of this integration no matter how unfavorable they may have been for Poland.

[40]Interestingly enough, a considerable degree of economic integration was also beginning to be achieved with Czechoslovakia even before it formally became a member of the communist system in 1948. After the war Czechoslovakia became one of Poland's most important trading partners. A number of important trade agreements were signed between the two states in this period, including the one of August 8, 1946, for the exchange of Polish electricity and Czechoslovakian goods and another in 1947 for the sale of Czech goods to Poland on credit.

the institution of state planning this centralization increased even further.

The flow of communications to and from the Soviet Union increased greatly, whereas that with other states decreased noticeably from what it had been before the war—both because of government policies and because of the wartime disruption of the economy, trade, tourism, and the social system.

Though integration with the communist world was by no means complete in this area, the volume of exchange between Poland and the U.S.S.R. was far higher than before the war, owing primarily to the enormous increase in the volume of Soviet books, periodicals, and radio broadcasts to Poland. The communications needs of trade and political control also contributed to this increase. The Polish and Soviet transport and communications networks were most closely integrated in both a formal and a real sense along the supply routes from the U.S.S.R. to Germany. Here, particularly, the U.S.S.R. controlled all decisions.

Communications with the other communist-ruled states and with Czechoslovakia also increased, though not nearly to the extent that this was true with the U.S.S.R. Toward the end of this period cultural cooperation agreements were signed with Yugoslavia (March 16, 1946—denounced in 1948), Bulgaria (June 28, 1947), Czechoslovakia (July 4, 1947), and later with Hungary (January 31, 1948), Rumania (February 27, 1948), the G.D.R. (January 8, 1950), and Albania (December 6, 1950).[41]

Communications with the West still continued in

___

[41] A cultural co-operation agreement similar to those signed with the other party states was later signed with the People's Republic of China (April 3, 1951).

this period, but the flow was considerably reduced from what it had been in the pre-entry period and gradually diminished relative to communication with the communist system. A Convention on Intellectual Co-operation, however, was signed with France on February 19, 1947.

The Socialization Subsystem. The postwar government placed great emphasis on education and educational opportunity for the workers and the peasants. In the schools there was much more technical and vocational training and adult education than there had been before the war. The government's "go-slow" policy, the shortage of qualified teachers, and lack of communist control over the classrooms ruled out a full scale program of indoctrination in Marxism-Leninism. The schools, however, were increasingly used to promote ideas and ideals favored by the Soviet and Polish communists. Praise of the new government and the role of the U.S.S.R. in liberating Poland and aiding in its reconstruction, for example, were themes that were emphasized more and more. In addition, the changed postwar situation understandably brought about new stress on the importance of practical work and social co-operation to rebuild the country, to re-affirm the traditional Polish character of the recovered territories and their significance to the Polish economy, and so forth. The new government also tried to distract attention from the adverse actions of the U.S.S.R. by emphasizing wartime destruction and atrocities committed by the Germans, thereby keeping alive the Polish anti-German feeling.

The communists, of course, also carried on their propaganda campaign outside the schools in an attempt to win support for the new government. Their control of the mass media was of key importance here. They also worked hard at training the new cadres of Party activists who had been recruited during and after the war.[42]

The Degree of Integration: Its Costs and Benefits

Aside from the Polish elite, who owed their elevation to power and continued exercise of it to the U.S.S.R., it seems fair to conclude that what integration there was in this period with the communist system was perceived as far more costly than beneficial by the Poles, particularly by the political and economic groups who were repressed or discriminated against. It is true that all the costs of integration—particularly the economic ones—were not then generally known to the population, but the nonmaterial costs alone were not hard to perceive: the imposition by a traditional enemy of an alien and generally unwanted socioeconomic and political system, the consequent loss of freedom in the selection of a government and the making of domestic and foreign policy accord-

[42]The Polish Workers' Party started with only 4,000 members in 1942 and had built its ranks to only 20,000 by mid-1944. After the Germans were driven out of Poland and a communist victory seemed likely, however, the growth of Party membership increased rapidly. By mid-1947 there were nearly 850,000 PPR members, most of whom had joined in the enthusiasm of victory and in the excitement of the reconstruction program. Few had any real Marxist-Leninist background. The Party also had to accept many who joined thinking that this was the most promising way to make a career for themselves or, at best, thinking that under the circumstances the Party was the most effective channel for making a contribution to their nation. For the most complete summary of the growth of the PPR and the PZPR see: Richard F. Staar, *Poland, 1944–1962* (Baton Rouge: Louisiana State U. Press, 1962).

ing to Polish interests, the widespread presence of Soviet troops and advisors, political turmoil and the disruption of the social order, and so forth.

In addition, however, there were a good many objective costs that did not become widely recognized until later, such as the unfavorable trade agreement (and in particular the coal agreement), the loss of German reparations payments, the Soviet veto of Polish participation in the Marshall Plan, increasing pressure to shift trade from the West to the communist world, and the loss of hundreds of thousands of skilled leaders, administrators, and technicians as a result of imprisonment or voluntary exile.

At the same time, it can also be argued that the few benefits to Poland as a result of integration within the communist world were also not then generally perceived by the population. The major objective benefit was probably military protection for the recovered territories, but this was not yet widely appreciated because of the weakened position of Germany at the time and the Polish distaste for having Soviet troops on Polish soil.

The potential positive psychological impact of the Soviet economic aid was offset by the loss of Marshall Plan aid and by the low quality and often inflated costs of the goods received. The Soviet technical advisors were also associated with the Soviet occupation forces, despite their important contributions to the Polish economy. Finally, the technical documentation agreement with the U.S.S.R. came late in this period and its full impact was not felt until the following period. Moreover, it can be argued that the documentation available from the U.S.S.R. was generally not up to date and underlined the costs, rather than the benefits, of integration with the communist system, though it seems unlikely that the long-range costs of reconstruction with obsolete equipment and technical documentation was fully or widely appreciated at the time.

The acquisition of the recovered territories—which could conceivably be counted as a consequence of integration with the U.S.S.R.—was perceived as beneficial, but its impact was offset by the loss of the land in the east to the U.S.S.R., even though the recovered territories were probably of much greater long-range value (something also not widely perceived at the time). Even assuming that without integration into the communist system the most popular of the social and economic reforms instituted after the war would not have been possible, probably only a minority understood the relationship between integration into the communist world (and Soviet backing of a Polish communist-dominated government) and these reforms. The war, noncommunist reform groups in the coalition government, and even patriotic Polish communists undoubtedly got more credit than the U.S.S.R. On the contrary, the Poles were quick to see the unpopular reforms and developments as resulting from Soviet interference and support for an unwanted communist government.

Although the general mass of the Polish population welcomed many of the social and economic reforms that took place in Poland after the war—and nearly everyone could agree with something in the program of the new government—there seems to have been no strong general desire for any integration with the Soviet Union, certainly not on the terms that emerged. There would have been little objection to increased trade relations with the U.S.S.R. and other communist-ruled states as long as the terms were favorable and as long as it was not at the expense of trade with the West. Political and military co-operation with the U.S.S.R. might have been more acceptable, too, in view of the tragic demonstration that distant allies offer little protection against neighboring enemies, but not at the expense of falling under the control of the U.S.S.R. and serving its interests instead of Polish ones. Likewise, most Poles had no objection to public ownership and social welfare, but few favored adopting the Soviet model of society or Soviet culture. After the communist take-over the Polish population may have considered integration into the communist system inevitable, but certainly not desirable.

Even the Polish communist elite and the growing number of people they were able to enlist in their support undoubtedly viewed extensive integration with the communist world as a mixed blessing at best. The communists certainly welcomed the Soviet aid in elevating them to power and helping to keep them there, but it seems unlikely that most of them were very enthusiastic about so much direct and indirect control by the Soviet Union and its agents in Poland. It may well be, however, that they felt it an inevitable or even a reasonable price to pay for staying in power or for transforming Poland into a socialist state.

In any case, there were certainly many points of conflict between the Soviet Union and at least a sizable proportion of the Polish communist leaders. The Soviet "factory-looting" operations in the recovered territories and the compulsory deliveries of coal to the U.S.S.R. were particularly unpopular among the Polish elite. It is also apparent that a significant group of the Polish communists differed with the Soviet leadership over the exact form that reconstructed Polish society should take and the means that should be used to bring about the change. In foreign policy most of the Polish elite apparently preferred closer economic ties with the West because of the greater economic benefits that were to be gained by such a relationship, if not also in order to keep Poland from being so dependent on the U.S.S.R. This view seems to have been confirmed by the initial Polish desire to participate in the Marshall Plan. In the consolidation period, however, any differences between the Poles and the Soviets were submerged in the joint effort to consolidate the communist position in Poland.

At this point neither the Polish elite nor the general population was in any position to effect any change in integration in the direction of their demands. It is likely that the degree of Polish opposition to Soviet demands for integration, however, prevented the costs to Poland from being higher than they were and the transition to the Soviet model of society from being any more rapid than it was. By the middle of this period whatever expectation there may have been that Poland could in the near future effect any change in the degree of integration or the basic character of the decisions made by the Soviet leadership had begun to fade. By the end of the period there were already signs that integration with the communist world was more likely to increase and that the degree of direct and indirect Soviet control and influence would become even greater.

3: THE PERIOD OF INTENSIVE SOCIALIST CONSTRUCTION, 1948–53[1]

Changes in the Environment

A number of significant changes in the international environment took place in this period, with important consequences for Poland's integration with the communist world. Most important was the intensification of the cold war as the uneasy postwar relationship between the U.S.S.R. and the Western allies began to deteriorate. The Soviet decision to strive for more intensive socialist development in the people's democracies and to tighten Moscow's control over

[1]The beginning of this period was marked by the intensification of the cold war, the entry of Czechoslovakia into the communist system, and the expulsion of Yugoslavia from the Cominform. The end of the period is more difficult to identify. In one sense it ended with the death of Stalin, who personally symbolized developments in Poland between 1948 and his death in 1953. In practice, however, the Stalinist period in Poland continued until 1955 when the first major effects of the thaw began to be felt. The description of Poland given in this section, therefore, is generally as true for 1954 and early 1955 as it is for the 1950–53 period.

The Soviet Union in this period achieved its greatest degree of control over Poland and applied the strongest pressure to intensify the speed of Poland's economic development and evolution toward a socialist society modeled after the U.S.S.R. It was, consequently, a period in which important changes took place within both Poland and the rest of the communist system.

domestic developments in eastern Europe, the organization of the Cominform (September-October, 1947), the expulsion of Yugoslavia from the international communist movement, and the communist coup in Czechoslovakia (February, 1948) were followed by a hardening of the Western position, the American policy of containment, and the formation of the NATO alliance (1949). The communist victory in China and the Korean War in 1950 further intensified the tension and hostility between the communist world and the West. In the economic field, the implementation of the Marshall Plan for the development of Europe and the Soviet refusal to allow the communist-ruled states of eastern Europe to participate led to the formation of the Council for Mutual Economic Assistance (January, 1949), which provided a communist substitute for the Marshall Plan. The emergence of two *de facto* German states was also of great importance in this period. The economic and political recovery of West Germany was of particular significance in view of the failure of the Western allies to recognize the Oder-Neisse boundary as permanent. The effect of these developments, together with the growth of Soviet military power following the development of their nuclear capability, made Poland and its communist elite increasingly dependent on the U.S.S.R. for protection from potential danger from the West.

Changes in the Belief System

For the mass of the population the basic elements of the belief system still remained largely the same, though gradually the communist control over communications and the constant propaganda about the superiority of socialism and the wonders and generosity of the Soviet Union were beginning to have their effect. Most people—including those within the Party —did not know the extent of the police terror and Soviet control over Poland or how costly economic integration with the communist system really was. With no other source of information except hearsay it is no wonder that so many—especially the young and the politically naive—began to believe what they heard from official sources. This was particularly understandable within the Party where there was such intensive indoctrination, so many additional pressures to believe, and such large rewards for doing so. It was also in this period that the highest degree of popular admiration for the U.S.S.R. and Soviet culture was achieved. Nevertheless, Poland on the whole still remained culturally oriented toward the West, despite this superficial change in attitude toward the U.S.S.R.

There was an increasingly sharp division between popular aspirations and official policies made by the members of the ruling elite. The popular demands of the previous period had now been supplemented by a desire to escape from the intensified police terror and Soviet control, to see the church allowed to continue its various activities without government repression, to see the standard of living rise more rapidly, and to have freedom of travel and contact with the West restored. There seemed little hope, however, that these objectives could be realized in the near future.

Poland achieved the greatest degree of cultural similarity to the Soviet Union and to the other communist-ruled states in this period. The new Polish Constitution of 1952 and the adoption of a Soviet-style system of local government brought the Polish governmental institutions more into line with those of the U.S.S.R. The continued existence of more than one party, the presence of a large number of front organizations, the strength of the Catholic church, and the relative failure of the drive to collectivize agriculture remained the major structural differences between Poland and the U.S.S.R.

In this period there were undoubtedly a growing number of people who had been won over to the idea that a society modeled after the U.S.S.R. would be the best for Poland, but the majority certainly still preferred a society that was more Polish and pluralistic and less Soviet and Marxist. Communist propaganda had been most effective among the youth and workers and probably least effective among the peasants who had been even more alienated by the collectivization drive at the beginning of this period.

Whatever their private feelings after the purge of Gomulka, the members of the PZPR hierarchy remained publicly united in their support of the Soviet line. It seems likely, however, that prudence rather than conviction persuaded a good many of them to support the Soviet position. No doubt the cold war and the fear of Western intervention also contributed to their willingness to go along with the U.S.S.R., as did their recognition that they needed Soviet backing to stay in power at home.

Changes in the Social System

The Political Subsystem. The most important changes in the political subsystem were the further tightening of Party control over the domestic political process, increased Soviet exercise of control over internal affairs in Poland, a narrowing of the range of deviation from the Soviet model, a virtual end to the earlier emphasis on a Polish road to socialism and the

close linkage between socialism and Polish nationalism, the beginning of a concerted attack on the Roman Catholic church, and a marked increase in police
terror.

More than ever the Party exercised complete control over the political process, virtually dispensing
with the need for the constitutionally established formal institutions of government. Within the Party
apparatus a duplicate government bureaucracy
emerged to supervise and direct the day-to-day operations of its government counterpart. In this period the
communists managed to eliminate or else penetrate
and control every major social and political institution that had not already fallen under its control—
with the one exception of the Roman Catholic
church.[2] In 1949 all major Polish youth groups

[2]The Polish communists, to be sure, did what they could to
weaken the Church and were not entirely without success. They
tried to divide the clergy with a movement of "patriot priests";
to woo the laity with "PAX" (see end of note); to secularize
the schools with the aid of the Association of Children's
Friends; to promote atheism through the Association of Atheism and Free Thinkers, the youth organizations, and the press;
to discourage Church attendance; to reduce the freedom of the
Church to make its own appointments; to curtail drastically the
Church-controlled press; to end religious instruction in the
schools; and, generally, to reduce the prestige and power of the
Church through the dissemination of antireligious propaganda,
the spread of secular education, the establishment of competing
organizations and forms of entertainment, and the opening of
the rural areas to urban and secular influences. Nevertheless,
despite communist successes, the Church was too deeply im-
bedded in traditional Polish culture and too strongly supported
by the population for the Party to bring it under its control or
seriously undermine its influence in this period. In fact, the
more the Church was attacked, the more the population went
to Church as a symbolic act of protest against the government.
For more details, see Adam Bromke, "From 'Falanga' to
'PAX'," *Survey*, (Dec., 1961) pp. 29–40; Gsovski, *Church and
State;* and Staar, *Poland.*

merged to create the Union of Polish Youth (ZMP). The December, 1948, union of the PPR and the PPS to form the Polish United Workers' Party (PZPR) was followed in November, 1949, by a merger of the communist-sponsored Peasant Party and the remnants of the PSL to form the United Peasant Party (ZSL). The following June the Democratic Party (SD) and the Labor Party (SP) joined under the Democratic Party (SD) name.

Other organizations in Poland were also consolidated and brought under closer Party control. In September, 1949, for example eleven patriotic organizations of veterans and former German war prisoners were united to form the politically important mass organization known as the Union of Fighters for Freedom and Democracy. The trade unions were also made more effective instruments for transmitting the decisions of the PZPR leadership.

Inside the PZPR itself the upper echelons of the organization continued to maintain complete control over Party activities and the mass of the Party members. A collective leadership at the Politburo level functioned as dictator over both the Party and the nation, though initiating policies of its own only within the limits set by Moscow. Increasingly the parties and other social institutions became one-way channels of communication and control, transmitting orders from the PZPR hierarchy to the Polish masses.

The Poles were kept informed of what was expected of them through their reading of the Soviet press and the Cominform journal, frequent meetings with representatives of the Soviet government and the CPSU, and contact with Soviet advisors and other agents of the U.S.S.R. and CPSU working in Poland. Although devotion to the communist cause and loyalty to the

U.S.S.R. may have been sufficient reason to obey for the most ardent Polish communists, their beliefs were reinforced by the fact that the military and secret police were still largely under Soviet control.

In 1948 the Soviet Union initiated a purge within the PZPR, supporting those within the Party who were willing to go along with the new Soviet hard line in domestic policy and international relations and demanding the removal of those, such as Gomulka and his supporters, who resisted the hard line in favor of a softer, more nationalistic, and slower approach to socialism. It is not entirely clear to what extent the victorious Party faction clearly felt that the Moscow line was ideologically and politically correct and to what extent it calculated that this was the only choice open to Poland in the face of overwhelming Soviet power. In any case, Gomulka and his supporters were purged, losing their Party and government posts and their PZPR membership. Though Gomulka and some of his most important supporters were imprisoned, there were no show trials or executions of former leaders as took place elsewhere in eastern Europe.

In addition to a purge of the top Party leadership, there was also an extensive purge of the lower echelons of the Party. The secret police became an increasingly important instrument for keeping both the masses and the Party members under control. The Soviet Union, in turn, used the secret police to keep the PZPR leadership under control.[3]

In short, the four years of communist rule had been

[3]For insight into the operation of the Polish political system in this period, see the scripts of the "Voice of America" radio broadcasts made by Lt. Col. Jozef Swiatlo in 1954–55 after his defection to the West from Poland, where he had worked in the secret police.

enough to win sufficient active and passive support in Poland so that it was possible for the Soviet Union and its Polish communist followers to dispense with the moderate and coalition character of the government and to proceed to build a more Soviet-style society, dropping those members who would not accept the change willingly.

The Party leaders in this period, however, were less dependent on direct support from the U.S.S.R. than they had been before, now that the organized opposition had been eliminated and an efficient network of communist control established. The ultimate threat of Soviet intervention, though, probably remained necessary to keep the communist elite in power and to effect the transformation of Polish society according to the Soviet model.

This was also the period in which the greatest degree of political and military integration was achieved, though much of it operated through informal channels. Politically the CPSU probably exercised no closer supervision than it had in the consolidation period, but its demands were more specific, and it required closer adherence to the Soviet model and the purge of those who expressed more moderate or nationalistic views. The means of control seem to have changed little from the previous period, though the secret police may have been used more extensively to keep the Polish elite under control.[4]

The Military Subsystem. In this period Poland began to become more dependent on the U.S.S.R. for

---

[4]Swiatlo, for example, revealed that even Boleslaw Bierut, Gomulka's successor as head of the PZPR, had a secret police dossier that was kept up to date. Swiatlo, "Voice of America," Interview No. 36 (July 8, 1955). See also Chap. IV, fn 3.

the defense of its recovered territories against a rapidly recovering Federal Republic of Germany. In addition, with the intensification of the cold war the Soviet Union decided to build up the Polish armed forces as a serious military organization. In late 1949 Marshal Rokossowski, an able Soviet military leader of Polish descent, was appointed Marshal of Poland, Minister of National Defense, Commander in Chief of the Armed Forces, and Deputy Premier. In May, 1950, he became a member of the PZPR Politburo. Under Rokossowski's leadership the military budget was increased, new Polish officers were recruited, a universal military training law was enacted (1950), the size of the armed forces was considerably increased, and their equipment, supply, and organization modernized and improved.

The greatest military build-up and highest armament expenditures came as a response to the Korean War, when Poland, like other members of the communist system, was expected to make its contribution to the military effort. The Polish armed forces probably reached its maximum size in 1953 when there were perhaps 300,000 to 400,000 men under arms, not counting those in the militia or the security corps. Although Polish officers held many high posts in this period, Soviet officers continued to occupy key positions. Those Polish officers considered unreliable were weeded out. Though the most important opposition elements had been eliminated, the Polish armed forces were still of questionable reliability in any showdown with the U.S.S.R.

In this period a great deal of attention was devoted to building up a compulsory paramilitary organization among the youth, called Service for Poland. Although it undertook some practical tasks of reconstruction (for example, rubble clearing and road building), its primary purpose was to provide political indoctrination and training in leadership and skills which had some military usefulness.

The Economic Subsystem.[5] The major economic emphasis in this period was not on integration with and specialization among the individual eastern European states, but rather on autarky, with each state developing the full range of industry and becoming as self-sufficient as possible—at least in production if not in raw materials, though considerable emphasis was put on the search for new supplies of raw materials. The long-range consequences of such autarkic economic policies were to become rather costly, though this was not widely perceived at the time. For the present every attempt was made to mobilize the enthusiasm of the population by emphasizing progress and modernization through industrialization, emulating the example of both the West and the U.S.S.R.

In 1948 a collectivization drive in the countryside

---

[5]For general surveys of Polish postwar economic developments in greater detail see: T. P. Alton, *Postwar Economic Planning in Poland* (New York: Columbia U. Press, 1955); Dorothy S. Douglas, *Transitional Economic Systems: The Polish-Czech Example* (London: Routledge and K. Paul, 1953); R. P. Rochlin, *Die Wirtschaft Polens von 1945 bis 1952* (Berlin: Deutsches Institut fur Wirtschaftsforschung, n.d.); Norman J. Pounds and Nicholas Spulber, *Resources and Planning in Eastern Europe,* Slavic and Eastern European Series, vol. 4 (Bloomington: Indiana U. Publications, 1957); Nicholas Spulber, *The Economics of Communist Eastern Europe* (New York: Technology Press and Wiley, 1957); W. Stankiewicz and J. Montias, *Institutional Changes in the Polish Economy* (New York: Mid-European Studies Center, 1955); and A. Zauberman, *Industrial Progress in Poland, Czechoslovakia, and E. Germany, 1937–1962* (London, 1962).

was begun. Despite extensive communist efforts, however, it never really achieved success. Only about 9.2 per cent of the agricultural land was ever collectivized, most of it in the newly settled recovered territories. Another 13.5 per cent of the agricultural land was in state farms.[6]

Almost all the remaining private enterprise was socialized in this period, except for some retail services and craftsmen. The Six Year Plan (1950–55) intensified the extensive industrialization drive aimed at making Poland a major industrial power following the autarkic Soviet model, with most investment concentrated in heavy industry at the expense of consumer goods and agriculture. Labor discipline was more strictly enforced and the work norms increased. Production began to rise considerably above prewar levels in nearly every area of the economy. Many new industries, such as shipbuilding and a wide variety of machine-producing industries, began to function well.

A large number of production plants were built and operated under Soviet license, including the Zeran automobile works in Warsaw and the new Nowa Huta steel complex near Cracow. Many other plants depended on the import of Soviet, Czech, or East German components. Polish factories also began to adopt Soviet industrial standards.

The standard of living for the population, however, did not rise, as most of the economic advances were directed toward reinvestment. In addition, the demands put on the Polish economy by increased mili-

[6]*Rocznik Statystyczny, 1956,* p. 143. For a survey of Polish agricultural developments in this period see: E. Koenig, "Collectivization in Czechoslovakia and Poland," *Collectivization of Agriculture in Eastern Europe,* ed. Irwin T. Sanders (Lexington, Ky.: U. of Kentucky Press, 1957), pp. 103–39.

tary spending during the Korean War were very expensive in terms of the costs of new investment and the disruption of the current Six Year Plan (1950–55). Poland, for example, began the production of jet fighters, radar, and other expensive equipment.[7]

Soviet economic exploitation continued as Poland received less favorable prices for many exports than it could have obtained if these goods had been sold in the West. The prices of Soviet goods were also often higher and the quality lower than for goods available elsewhere. The proportion of Polish trade with the communist system continued to rise, however, reaching nearly 72 per cent in 1953, with a full 33.5 per cent of total Polish trade accounted for by the U.S.S.R. The G.D.R. (German Democratic Republic) absorbed another 15 per cent and Czechoslovakia 11 per cent.[8] [See Tables 3–5 in the Appendix.] As Poland industrialized, it became more and more dependent on the U.S.S.R. and the rest of the communist world for both capital goods and raw materials. An increasing proportion of Polish imports consisted of oil, iron and manganese ores, machinery, and grain.[9] The proportion of Polish exports of manufactured goods grew, whereas that of food products and raw materials declined. Great Britain (.7.4 per cent),

[7]It is estimated that about 11 per cent of total Polish industrial investment in the 1951–55 period went for military purposes. See Kaser, *COMECON*, p. 19.

[8]*Rocznik Statystyczny, 1959*, p. 252.

[9]Almost all of Poland's imports of these products came from the U.S.S.R., with the exception of machinery. Czechoslovakia provided most of the machinery imports, followed by the U.S.S.R. and the G.D.R. The U.S.S.R. provided all of Poland's manganese ore, nearly all its grain and cotton, and the great bulk of its oil and iron ore.

Sweden (3.0 per cent), and Finland (2.7 per cent) were its only significant trading partners outside the communist world.[10]

It is important to remember that the decline in trade with the West was due not only to increased pressures to trade with the other members of the communist system, but also largely to strategic controls, credit constrictions, and quotas that were imposed by the West as a result of the intensification of the cold war. The elimination of many Western sources of vital goods underlined the importance of technological progress and the achievement of self-sufficiency on the part of the communist world in general and the individual eastern European states in particular.

The nature of the developments in this period in Polish industry ultimately made the Polish economy more dependent on the U.S.S.R. and the other communist-ruled states despite the emphasis on autarky. Autarky was, in fact, impossible for Poland, given her limited raw materials and technological base. Though the Council for Mutual Economic Assistance (CMEA) was founded in January, 1949, as the communist answer to the Marshall Plan, it in fact did little in this period except provide a more formal channel for co-ordinating and standardizing bilateral trade agreements between the states of the communist system.[11] The Soviet Union, of course, had the

[10]Great Britain was still Poland's second most important trading partner as late as 1949 (11.8 per cent).

[11]In 1951 the CMEA members agreed on a Uniform Foreign Trade Contract, eliminating the need to negotiate separately conditions of delivery, quality of goods, packing, guarantees, payments, and arbitration each time a trade agreement was made. Kaser, *COMECON,* p. 49.

final say in determining the substance of the agreements to which it was a party.[12] By isolating Poland's economy from the West and its technology, new materials, and markets, Poland became increasingly tied to the CMEA economies and less suited to trade with the more developed West.

The Communications Subsystem. This period was the high point for communications integration with the U.S.S.R. and the rest of the communist system. The proportion of Polish communications with the West decreased to almost nothing. Western radio broadcasts were systematically jammed. The flow of tourists in both directions was nearly stopped. Western books, magazines, newspapers and films were seldom available, except for those carefully selected to serve the communists' purpose. Diplomatic relations with Western nations—particularly with the United States—were limited and severely strained. Imports of Soviet books, periodicals, films, plays, and so forth, increased markedly. Official Party and government communications were more and more oriented toward glorification of the U.S.S.R. Polish communications with the other party states were limited largely to the exchange of films and periodicals, and personal contacts between them were severely restricted. The U.S.S.R. became the co-ordinating hub through which communications flowed and were controlled.

Internally, censorship became more and more

[12]By 1954 multilateral trade links had been established between the G.D.R. and the other CMEA members, but Poland chose to abstain from such ties. In 1954 Hungary began to engage in joint industrial enterprises with Czechoslovakia and Rumania—in aluminum and chemicals, respectively—but Poland was slow to show an interest in such arrangements.

severe as pro-Soviet, prosocialist, hard-line propaganda became the rule, much of it originating in the Soviet Union. Anything not in accord with Soviet policies was censored and suppressed. The domestic communications pattern was based on directives from the central Party apparatus, operating outward and downward with some feedback to the center as a check on the success with which their orders had been carried out.

The Socialization Subsystem. The drive continued to build up the educational facilities of the country. At the same time, a much more intensive program of political indoctrination was introduced into the school program. This school indoctrination was supplemented by the programs of a large number of organizations for youth and adults outside the schools and in the factories and other places of work. An attempt was made to see that everyone was a member of at least one organization. Outside the organizational framework the mass media were fully mobilized to promote communist ideology and encourage hard work for economic development. Rigid censorship insured that information embarrassing to the communists would not reach the public.

Except for a temporary lull after the 1950 church-state accord, increasing pressure was brought to bear on the church in order to restrict its influence among the youth. Religious instruction was abolished in the schools; the church press was gradually restricted and its major organ, *Tygodnik Powszechny,* turned over to PAX (a religious organization that collaborated with the communists); and antireligious propaganda was intensified.

The Degree of Integration: Its Costs and Benefits

The major benefits of integration in this period were felt largely by the members of the Party elite who stood to lose their positions without it. The costs, however, were enormous. Coal deliveries continued to the Soviet Union, as did shipments of other goods, all at prices lower than those for which they could have been sold in the West. Likewise, the quality of the machinery and goods received in return was often lower than that which could have been obtained outside the communist world.[13] In addition, orders were lost from the West—in shipbuilding, for example —because Soviet orders took up the entire export production capacity of a given plant or industry. There were other kinds of costs as well. For example, Poland built a shipyard for the express purpose of producing a type of ship ordered by the U.S.S.R. only to have the order canceled about the time the yard was ready for production. Poland was also forced to drop its license arrangement with Fiat at considerable expense and to begin producing inferior cars under a Soviet license. Most expensive in many ways, however, was the pressure on Poland to increase its military expenditures during the Korean War.

There were also great additional intangible costs in this period resulting from the restrictions placed on freedom of expression, forced agricultural collectivization, the socialization of much of the remaining pri-

[13]Some of these costs were indirect results of integration into the communist system. Political and military integration into the system also resulted in western trade restrictions on the export of certain machines and goods badly needed for Poland's economic development program, thereby giving Poland no other alternative but economic integration with the system.

vate enterprise, errors in planning, the crash program of economic development according to the Soviet model, police terror, and the attacks on the church.

On the whole, there seems to have been little agreement in Poland with the nature of the existing integration with the U.S.S.R. and the rest of the communist system, except possibly inside Party circles. Even there, however, there seem to have been reservations about the forms that this integration took and its cost to Poland, particularly in the area of trade.

One mitigating factor in this period was that the enormous economic costs to Poland were still not known to the bulk of the population or even to many intellectuals and party members. Nor were the errors in economic planning yet widely understood. Though it is debatable whether Poland's economy really benefited from the change in the economic system which was imposed by the U.S.S.R. and the PZPR, it is clear that many Poles—especially the youth and those closest to the Party—perceived, at least for a few years, that the rapid pace of industrialization was of real benefit to the country. For the moment, the communists' control of the news, propaganda about rapid industrialization with enormous economic benefits for all in the near future, and police terror were sufficient to keep people from openly expressing their dissatisfaction. In addition the years of propaganda had created a slowly growing segment of the population which looked with favor on the new policies.

4: THE THAW, 1954–57[1]

Though its effects were not immediately felt in Poland, the death of Stalin and the resulting changes it brought about in the Soviet Union ushered in a new period for the Poles. Although there were relaxations in work discipline and in the tempo of industrialization in 1953 and 1954, this was probably more the result of economic necessity in Poland than a direct result of Stalin's death, and it was not until 1955 that the thaw was really apparent. Because the Poland of 1953–55 was so much like the Poland of 1949–53, the analysis in this section concentrates on the post-1955 part of the period.

[1]For some accounts of the thaw see: K. S. Karol, *Visa for Poland*, trans. Marvyn Savill (London: Macgibbon and Kee, 1959); Flora Lewis, *The Polish Volcano: A Case History of Hope* (London: Secker and Warburg, 1959); S. L. Schneiderman, *The Warsaw Heresy* (New York: Horizon Press, 1959); Konrad Syrop, *Spring in October: The Polish Revolution of 1956* (London: Weidenfeld and Nicolsen, 1957); and Paul E. Zinner, ed., *National Communism and Popular Revolt in Eastern Europe* (New York: Columbia U. Press, 1956). For a more recent analysis see: R. F. Staar, "Destalinization in Eastern Europe: The Polish Model," *Issues of World Communism*, ed. Andrew Gyorgy (Princeton, N.J.: Van Nostrand, 1966).

Changes in the Environment

The developments that took place in the external environment in this period were of extreme importance in making possible both the Polish thaw and the changes in Poland's relationship to the communist system. The most important changes in this respect were those in the Soviet Union resulting from the death of Stalin and the ensuing struggle for power in which Khrushchev eventually emerged as the most powerful man in the Soviet hierarchy. The Soviet reconciliation with Yugoslavia (1955), Khrushchev's destalinization speech (February, 1956), the dissolution of the Cominform (April, 1956), and China's growing power and prestige were also of great importance. All these developments worked together to create an atmosphere of uncertainty and instability in the communist world, to weaken the Soviet ability to serve as the unquestioned decision-maker for the communist system, and to encourage the other member states to assert themselves and act more independently. Other developments such as the Hungarian Uprising (November, 1956), growing discontent in other communist-ruled states, the resurgence of the western European economy and the prospects for the establishment of a west European common market, and growing economic needs within the communist system were important considerations in the 1956 Soviet decision to revitalize CMEA and make it an organization better suited to meet the mutual needs of the communist-ruled states of eastern Europe. The success of NATO and the very real spectre of a rearmed Federal Republic of Germany were also significant in bringing about the formation of the Warsaw Pact (May, 1955).

Changes in the Belief System[2]

The first part of this period was marked by slowly growing demoralization and disillusionment about the capacity of the existing government to fulfill its promises or satisfy the needs of the nation. The Swiatlo revelations[3] and Khrushchev's anti-Stalin speech of February, 1956, which was read at open Party meetings in Poland and generally became public knowledge, made a particularly great impact on Party and public morale.[4] It was not until the intellectuals had roused the public in 1955 and 1956 through the press and face-to-face discussions, however, that any sizable group of people really believed things might be changed.

Everyone had some sort of demand to make against the government. The intellectuals wanted more freedom of expression, honesty of criticism, and more

[2]For an anthology of contemporary Polish writing in this period see: Pawel Mayewski, ed., *The Broken Mirror: A Collection of Writings from Contemporary Poland* (New York: Random House, 1958).

[3]One of the major events that triggered the Polish thaw was the defection of Lieutenant Colonel Swiatlo of the Polish Secret Police in December, 1953, and his broadcasts to Poland over the "Voice of America" in late 1954 and 1955, telling of the full extent of the Soviet control over Poland and of the activities of the secret police. There had been rumors of such things, but the Swiatlo revelations, particularly since they were not denied by the government, not only confirmed them but also spread the knowledge of their existence.

[4]See, for example, Gozdzik's description of the reaction of the workers in a Warsaw automobile plant: "Tell the Truth! This is How Everything Started!," *Nowa Kultura* (Oct. 20, 1957), also translated and quoted in Adolf Sturmthal, "Workers' Councils in Poland," *Industrial and Labor Relations Review,* 14 (April, 1961), 379–96.

variety in cultural life; the workers wanted higher wages, lower norms, and better working conditions; the peasants wanted lower compulsory delivery quotas, higher prices for their products, and an end to the collectivization drive; most people wanted freer travel, more contact with the West, an end to the persecution of the Catholic church, more favorable economic relations with the other communist-ruled states, and more independence from Soviet control.

The communist leadership was split on most of these issues. Their differences stemmed from two major sources: first, there was disagreement on ideological grounds about the extent to which Polish society should differ from Soviet society—both in the short run and in the long run; second, the leadership differed in their judgments on just how far the Polish communists could go in pursuing more liberal policies without risking a popular uprising and Soviet intervention.

After the Poznan riots, however, more and more Party members agreed that some concessions to popular demands were necessary to gain the people's confidence, to avoid further disillusionment and apathy, and even to prevent a general uprising. Party intellectuals and domestically oriented leaders at the national level tended to be in favor of reform, with the more timid provincial leadership and the Moscow-trained communists favoring a harder position. The group that advocated change was able to win by effectively mobilizing the support of the workers, intellectuals, students, and key military units.

The major effects of the thaw narrowed the great gulf that had existed between the Party and the population and made the Polish people—both inside and outside the Party—more skeptical of communist promises. Although there were some strong popular demands for an end to communism in Poland and for Polish withdrawal from the communist system in late 1956, it soon became apparent in the wake of the Soviet suppression of the Hungarian uprising that the U.S.S.R. was not likely to sit idly by and see the third largest member of the communist system, and the key buffer state and supply route between itself and Germany, escape its control and fall into the hands of the NATO powers.

In the cultural sphere there seems to have been increasing divergence between Poland and the U.S.S.R., particularly as Western-style music, art, and literature became increasingly popular, even within Polish Party circles. In addition, the age of blind faith in communism had ended for most believers. A growing number of Party members probably also had their doubts about whether communism was either inevitable or desirable in Poland and would have been more than willing to settle for a socialist system.

It is also worth noting that Soviet and Polish communist thought deviated on another point—and probably always had: most Polish Party members did not share the Soviet enthusiasm for spreading communism or aiding the underdeveloped areas of the world. They were not really opposed to this, but they simply did not choose to devote many resources to such activities when there was so much yet to be done at home.

Changes in the Social System

The Political Subsystem. During this period the Party continued to control Poland, though after 1955 its control was neither as firm nor as certain as it had been during the previous six years; for a few brief weeks in 1956 there was no certainty that it could maintain control in the wake of the successful controversial discussions with the Soviet leaders in October, the PZPR concessions to popular demands, and the Soviet intervention in Hungary. Once the Hungarian crisis was over, however, the PZPR, under the leadership of Gomulka, consolidated its position and undisputably re-established effective control.

In 1956 the Poles presented a unified front and had managed to win considerable independence from Soviet control in both domestic and foreign policy. Not only had the Soviets been forced to remove specific instruments of control, such as their secret police agents and military officers and advisors, but the Poles had also won more latitude in adopting deviant domestic policies without risking Soviet intervention. They had also convinced the U.S.S.R. that it would have to take Polish interests more into account when making decisions that affected Poland. By being united and in control of their own military units the Poles were in a better position to bargain in the future as well. Even though the Soviet Union was overwhelmingly more powerful, the Poles were able to offer at least stiff, expensive, and embarrassing resistance that could invite Western intervention.

After 1956, Polish social institutions began to deviate even more from the Soviet model and the other communist states. For the moment, however, this deviation seemed to have at least the tacit approval of the U.S.S.R.

The Sejm, which had become virtually a dead body after 1947, once more began to carry on meaningful debate in the spring of 1956, though continued communist control of the Sejm and the law-making process kept it from becoming much more than a channel for the articulation of popular interests. (At the most its moderate, noncommunist deputies could argue for modification of the laws proposed by the communist-controlled Council of State.) In the 1957 elections, even a group of liberal Catholics were allotted a few seats in the Sejm by the communists (who still carefully controlled the election machinery).[5]

It was within the PZPR, however, that the most crucial changes took place. In the wake of Stalin's death the PZPR had been following a wait-and-see policy, but the 1954 Swiatlo revelations forced the Party to "democratize" the secret police, curbing its extralegal activities and bringing it more directly under Party control. At the same time the demoralization within the Party which had resulted from the Swiatlo revelations and growing popular dissatisfaction over low wages and shortage of consumer goods made it necessary for the Party to reconsider its basic program and offer some serious criticism for the first time since 1948. Khrushchev's anti-Stalin speech in February, 1956, added further to the doubt and unrest within the Party. The PZPR membership was divided, with the majority of the leadership afraid to initiate too radical a change lest it trigger an uncontrollable reaction. Some minor concessions were made to the workers, but they were inadequate to meet popular demands.

It was not until after the Poznan riots of June, 1956, that the Party was forced to act as well as to criticize. It became clear to almost everyone that the situation could not continue as it was. The Party

[5]For more information in the "Znak" group that was represented in the Sejm, see: Adam Bromke, "The 'Znak' Group in Poland," *East Europe*, 11 (Jan., 1962), 14–20.

had either to clamp down severely with the risk of further alienating the people or drastically relax its administration with the danger that things would get out of control and invite intervention. After some complex and dramatic behind-the-scenes Party debate and maneuvering, Gomulka was finally asked to return to power as First Secretary of the PZPR. It was widely believed that he was the only person who could unite the Party and the nation and keep the thaw from getting out of hand. After a dramatic and apparently controversial session with Khrushchev and an impressive delegation of Soviet leaders who visited Poland in October, Gomulka and his policy of reform were accepted by the U.S.S.R., and a Soviet promise was made to negotiate Polish grievances in trade and military policy.

Within the Party the thaw resulted in a much greater degree of democratization, greater freedom to criticize and make suggestions, and a greater degree of upward communication from the lower echelons of the Party. Outside the Party the major political change was more freedom to talk and criticize. Political discussion groups sprang up all over Poland.[6] Censorship was relaxed, and the press became more lively and interesting.

Between 1955 and 1957 the writers and other intellectuals gained a significant degree of influence, both inside and outside the Party. The influence of the liberal intellectuals was particularly great because of the control they had gained over many of the important periodicals. There was also more freedom to choose from a wider selection of music, art, and literature. Cardinal Wyszynski, who had been under detention

---

[6]See Witold Jedlicki, "The Crooked Circle Club," *East Europe*, 12 (June, 1963), 2–7.

since September 28, 1953, was restored to his position as head of the Catholic church in Poland, and the church regained the privilege of conducting classes in religious education in the schools and of publishing its own periodicals again.

After the 1956 showdown with the U.S.S.R., when the Polish leadership apparently stood united in the face of Soviet threats, the PZPR exercised almost complete independence in domestic policy and to some extent in foreign policy. The basic relationship with the communist world was not really changed, however, nor was the fundamental reality of ultimate Soviet control. What did change, though, were the limits within which the Polish communists were free to act. In domestic policy these limits were broad enough so that there was only a small gap between what the PZPR wanted and what the CPSU was willing to allow. The gap in foreign policy was wider, but the Soviet leaders had come to the realization that hereafter Poland could not simply be ordered around, but had to be treated as an equal sovereign state and offered greater benefits for its integration into the communist system.

The Military Subsystem. Though still remaining high, military expenditures were reduced after 1953, and the number of troops under arms gradually decreased. Until 1956 a large measure of control over the Polish military still rested in Soviet hands. In October, 1956, however, the Polish soldiers and officers rallied in support of the Polish Party leaders in their showdown with the Soviets and refused to obey their Russian superiors. Part of the Polish post-October agreement with the U.S.S.R. called for the recall of the thousands of Soviet officers and advisors, who were subsequently replaced by regular Polish officers. Rokossowski was dismissed from his military duties, dropped from his government and Party functions, and sent back to the U.S.S.R. in late 1956. Poland also managed to obtain a status of forces agreement with the Soviet Union, theoretically giving the Poles control over the Soviet troop movements within Poland as well as the right to try Soviet soldiers in Polish courts for off-duty crimes.[7]

In May, 1955, Poland joined with the other communist-ruled states of East Europe (except Yugoslavia) to form the Warsaw Pact. There is little evidence that this treaty really altered the pattern of integration of the Polish forces into the communist military system, though it may have formalized some of the previously existing informal channels of control and brought consultation a little more out in the open. Having these more formal channels of consultation may, however, have been of considerable importance in maintaining Polish military integration with the other communist-ruled states after the dismissal of the Soviet officers in 1956.[8]

Because of an increasing popular opposition in Poland in the early part of this period, the Polish leadership became more and more dependent on force and the threat of Soviet intervention to maintain their position. From June to December, 1956, the threat of imminent Soviet intervention was particularly important for the Polish elite, but became less so during 1957. It

[7]See: "Agreement on the Legal Status of Soviet Troops," *American Journal of International Law,* 52 (Jan., 1958), 221–27.

[8]For more information on the Warsaw Pact see: R. F. Staar, "The East European Alliance System," *Proceedings of the U.S. Naval Institute,* 90 (Sept., 1964), 26–39.

is worth noting, however, that after the failure of the Hungarian uprising, the threat of ultimate Soviet intervention probably allowed the Polish communists to maintain their position with less resort to force and repression than would have otherwise been the case. In addition, with the advent of a rearmed Federal Republic of Germany, Polish dependence on the U.S.S.R. for military protection for its recovered territories continued to increase, especially in view of the continued failure of the Western powers to recognize the Oder-Neisse boundary as final.

The Economic Subsystem.[9] Before October, 1956, unsuccessful attempts had been made to increase lagging agricultural production by lowering compulsory deliveries. After October, however, the PZPR returned to its pre-1948 agricultural policy, further reduced compulsory deliveries, raised prices, increased investment in the agricultural sector, and allowed the peasants who wanted to do so to disband their collective farms. The number of families in collectives dropped from a high of 188,500 in 1955 to 27,000 by the end of 1956.[10]

The industrialization drive continued, with its emphasis on producer's goods, but there was some investment cutback and relaxation of work norms after 1953. In 1956 the workers were given a raise in pay, and the government recognized the legitimacy of the workers' councils that had sprung up spontaneously in the previous months.[11] More attention was also paid

[9]See Spulber, *Resources and Planning* and John Montias, "Unbinding the Polish Economy," *Foreign Affairs*, 35 (April, 1957), 470–84. See also: Zauberman, *Industrial Progress.*

[10]*Rocznik Statystyczny, 1960,* p. 220.

[11]See Sturmthal, "Workers' Councils in Poland," pp. 379–96.

to the production of consumer's goods, but this was too late to avoid inflation resulting from the wage increases granted for political reasons. At the same time the PZPR returned to its early policy on private enterprise. The state even began to offer loans and technical advice to private businessmen if the government felt the proposed enterprise met a real economic need.[12]

A number of important developments in the structure of formal relationships between the member states of the communist system took place in this period. In early 1955 the U.S.S.R. agreed to supply Poland and each of the other CMEA members (except Albania) with a nuclear reactor. In March of the following year the United Institute for Nuclear Research was established in Dubna (in the U.S.S.R.) with the participation of all the European and Asian communist-ruled states (except Yugoslavia).[13] A network of technical collaboration treaties was signed by the CMEA states, further expanding the exchange of technical documentation. Formal discussion began on rail co-operation, leading to the formation of the Organization for Railway Co-operation in June, 1956.[14] In September of the following year the formal treaty was signed by all the communist-ruled states (except Yugoslavia). That same year agreement was reached

[12]See: J. Przybla, "Private Enterprise in Poland Under Gomulka," *American Slavic Review,* 17 (Oct., 1958), 316–31; and James F. Morrison, "The Private Road to the Top in People's Poland," *Sequoia,* 7 (Autumn, 1961), 14–23 and (Winter, 1962), 44–52.

[13]North Vietnam was not an original member but joined before the end of 1956.

[14]Poland and Czechoslovakia also maintained their long-standing membership in the International Union of Railroads founded in 1922.

on the establishment of a new scheme for a multi-lateral clearing house to facilitate trade among CMEA members. At the end of 1957 the Organization for the Co-operation of the Socialist Countries in Telecommunications and Posts was established, again including all the communist-ruled states except Yugoslavia. In 1958 an agreement was reached on a power grid linking the CMEA states, though it was not effected until 1962. There were also discussions in 1958 on the construction of an oil pipeline to supply Soviet oil to Poland, Czechoslovakia, and the G.D.R., though the formal agreement was not signed until 1959.

There is every reason to believe that the Polish government after 1956 was one of the strongest supporters of a revitalized CMEA. The Poles were particularly concerned about the expansion of their markets in the communist world, particularly after the formation of the European Common Market in 1957 threatened to eliminate many of Poland's traditional markets in the West. Technical collaboration, a multi-lateral clearing scheme, and rational and equitable specialization of production through the co-ordination of long-range plans all promised substantial economic benefits to Poland. At the same time the Poles were successfully negotiating for greater decentralization of co-operative endeavors and for equality in negotiation and economic bargaining with the U.S.S.R., essential conditions for making a revitalized CMEA attractive to all the eastern European states.

One other area in which the Poles were successful was their 1956–57 support for bilateral and multilateral sharing of investment costs on major projects of benefit to other CMEA states. Particularly in the area of mineral exploitation, where there was a growing need in the communist world for raw materials—and where the Poles had considerable export potential—but where initial investment costs were high and required several years before there were returns, the Poles argued that the states most interested in the potential minerals should share in financing the initial investment. CMEA approved the idea, and the first such decentralized credit arrangement was a G.D.R. investment of 25 million dollars in Polish coal mining to be repaid in kind after the new mines began operation. This was followed by a similar Czech investment of 63 million dollars in Polish coal mining near the Czech border. The Czechs also agreed to invest 25 million dollars in Polish sulphur exploitation.[15] In addition the Poles and Czechs agreed on provisions for decentralized contacts between various technical and administrative agencies of the two states. The agreement served as a precursor for an entire network of Intergovernmental Commissions on Economic, Scientific, and Technical Collaboration which was to spring up between the CMEA states in the next few years.[16]

This continuing industrialization increased Poland's dependence on the import of raw materials. The nature of the industrialization made Poland particularly dependent on the Soviet Union for raw materials and markets for certain plants geared specifi-

---

[15]Poland, Czechoslovakia, and the G.D.R. also shared in financing the costs of a new paper mill complex in Rumania. Subsequently, there were other such economic arrangements, including a Czech investment in Polish copper mining (1961) and in a major fertilizer plant at Pulawy, Polish and Hungarian investment in the exploitation of Soviet phosphates (1962), and so forth.

[16]Poland subsequently signed Intergovernmental Commissions on Economic, Scientific, and Technical Collaboration agreements with Czechoslovakia (1957), Bulgaria (1958), Hungary (1958), Rumania (1958), the G.D.R. (1960), and the U.S.S.R. (1964).

cally to Soviet resources and needs. Although the proportion of Polish trade with the communist world declined to 64.9 per cent in 1955 and even further (to 62.2 per cent) by 1957, the Soviet Union still accounted for 33.7 per cent of Poland's imports and 26.5 per cent of its exports in 1957. [See Tables 3 and 4 in the Appendix.] The Federal Republic of Germany, the United States, France, and the underdeveloped countries were the main states outside the communist system to absorb the remainder of Polish trade. Poland became an observer in GATT in 1957 and showed strong interest in expanding her trade with the West.

The Soviet Union continued to receive some isolated price advantages after 1956, but for the most part the terms of trade were much fairer—at least if one ignores the question of quality, reliability of delivery, and choice of goods available. One of the most important developments in Polish-Soviet trade was the Soviet agreement in late 1956 to end the compulsory coal deliveries. As important as this was, Poland could not take full advantage of its new export potential because there was a sharp drop in the world price of coal at about the same time. The Soviet Union, however, agreed to cancel the entire Polish debt of 525 million dollars in exchange for settlement of Polish claims for uncollected German reparations and the unfair prices in the coal-delivery agreement. In addition, Poland received a loan of 700 million rubles and a two-year credit for 1.4 million tons of wheat.[17]

Poland also received some credits from the West in

[17]In February, 1957, Poland extended $10,000,000 in credits to Hungary, following the lead of the U.S.S.R., Bulgaria, the G.D.R., and China. Czechoslovakia and the U.S.S.R. extended further credits to Hungary in March. (See Kaser, *COMECON*, pp. 69–70.)

1957: 10 billion francs from France, 9 million dollars from the Federal Republic of Germany, and 95 million dollars from the United States (including 30 million dollars from the Export-Import Bank to be repaid in dollars in twenty yearly installments, beginning in 1962, and 65 million dollars for the purchase of surplus farm commodities on even more favorable terms).

The Communications Subsystem. The most important development in the early part of this period was the relaxation of censorship in 1955, permitting more criticism and an honest exchange of ideas. In this area, too, the Polish elite had regained control, with the more liberal elements in the Party leadership having wrested control of the Party and government from those who supported tighter controls over communications and the orthodox Soviet view in cultural affairs. After June, 1956, the jamming of Western radio broadcasts was ended and other channels of communication with the West began to open up again, including the beginnings of a rapid growth in the number of tourists coming to Poland.

It is also worth noting that physical communications facilities in Poland improved enormously during this and the preceding period, particularly in the countryside. Electrification of the villages brought unprecedented contact between the peasants and the rest of the nation, particularly through the radio. New libraries, bus lines, telephones, and movie theaters also provided new channels for drawing the villagers into national life—and for putting them in contact with communist propaganda.

After 1955–56 Poland once again began to exchange communications in significant quantities with states outside the communist system. The volume of both communications and travel increased steadily (and continued to do so well into the next period). In addition, the volume of communications and the number of official contacts with the other states of eastern Europe also increased considerably above what had been the norm for the previous period and the early part of this one. [See Table 11 in the Appendix.]

Government information control and censorship, however, still favored the U.S.S.R. and the official Polish communist views in domestic and foreign policy. Travel to and communications from the West were still restricted, both because of a shortage of foreign exchange for travel and the purchase of Western mass media and because many of the Polish Party leaders believed that unlimited contact with the West would be undesirable.

The Socialization Subsystem. After 1956 the content of both school instruction and the mass media became far more objective and less dogmatic. Admission to the universities depended more on merit and less on political loyalty and family background. Religious education was reintroduced in the schools. There was much more contact with Western and noncommunist ideas, art, music, drama, films, and literature than had been true during the Stalinist period, when most of the contact was through the officially controlled media. The Polish press, in becoming a meaningful medium for the expression of criticism and controversial ideas, did much to stimulate an atmosphere of ferment and change. As a result of this stimulation and the earlier relaxation of police terror, the coffee houses and other informal meeting places quickly developed into animated forums, alive with discussion and debate, and soon became some of the most important institutions in the socialization process, further reducing the Party's control over this fundamental social process.

The Degree of Integration: Its Costs and Benefits

By 1956 the same kind of costs were incurred by Poland as in previous years. However, the Swiatlo revelations of late 1954 and the growing number of open criticisms by the intellectuals made people aware of many of these costs for the first time. Disadvantageous trade relations with the U.S.S.R. continued until 1956, as did the compulsory coal deliveries. In addition, the direction of Polish industrialization had also added to the costs of integration by making Poland dependent on the U.S.S.R. for many raw materials and markets. Some of the Polish steel and textile mills, in fact, were designed specifically to use Soviet ores and raw cotton. Certain plants and shipyards were built to produce specific products that were needed only in the U.S.S.R., thereby contributing to the inflexibility of the Polish economy and the potential cost of expensive idleness or conversion to other production in case supplies of raw materials should break down or orders be canceled. This obviously also made Poland much more subject to political pressure from the U.S.S.R.

After 1956 the worst costs of integration were eliminated, but Poland was still subject to the continued threat of ultimate Soviet intervention, economic dependence on the U.S.S.R., pressures to trade with the members of the communist system, the lack of complete Polish freedom in foreign policy, and general Soviet support for a government and policies that would not otherwise have been accepted by the general population. The Soviet Union still continued to receive some isolated price advantages in its trade with Poland after 1956, but on the whole the terms of trade were fairer. In fact, Poland received more favorable terms of trade in its exchanges with the U.S.S.R. and the other communist-ruled states than it did in its exchanges with the West, though many of these superficial price advantages were probably more than offset by the costs of having to accept unwanted or substandard products, a narrower choice of goods, unpredictable delivery dates, difficulties in getting spare parts and replacements, and so forth.[18]

Poland's major benefit from integration remained the defense of territories recovered from the Germans; this was increasingly perceived as important as a powerful Federal German Republic began to emerge and as many of its citizens and leaders began to proclaim publicly their desire to recover their lost territories. The PZPR was not slow in taking advantage of such statements.

The impact of Khrushchev's Twentieth Party Congress speech was particularly great for members of the PZPR. Although some of the wrongs of the Stalinist period were acknowledged and eventually corrected (for example, the rehabilitation of the prewar Polish Communist Party and the release of most of the Polish communists imprisoned between 1948 and 1956), it was a terrible disillusionment for most sincere and loyal Party members to become aware for the first time of the real costs of integration for both the Party and nation, and to see that all the wrongs had not yet been corrected.

After 1956, however, the costs of integration for the

[18]See: Frederic L. Pryor, *The Communist Foreign Trade System* (Cambridge: M.I.T. Press, 1963), pp. 172–80.

Party members were very small, and a revitalized and reorganized CMEA promised to provide substantial benefits. Moreover, the PZPR still received indirect support for its position of power from the ultimate threat of Soviet intervention. There is also evidence that the Polish elite, committed to remaining within the communist system and recognizing their dependence upon it, saw considerable economic advantages for Poland through the revitalization of CMEA, making it an organization for real mutual economic assistance and co-operation in which there would be room for negotiation and agreements based on mutual advantage. Moreover, by revitalizing CMEA there would be a sounder basis for stability within the communist system. (It is important to remember that although the PZPR leaders may have been interested in increasing Poland's independence within the communist system, providing greater benefits for their state, and increasing the range of choice open to them, there is no evidence that they wished to leave the system.) For the PZPR and its supporters the benefits of integration clearly exceeded the costs after 1956.

For most Poles, however, the costs of integration—though now more tolerable—were still too high. The bulk of the people still preferred an even less Soviet-style society, even more independence from the U.S.S.R., more trade and closer relations with the West, more personal freedom of travel and expression, and a slower pace of economic development with more immediate benefits. The general population, however, tended to perceive and rationalize most of the costs of integration in this period as stemming not so much from integration into the communist world as from having the misfortune of being on the east side of Germany, thus making the integration inevitable. Moreover, most Poles initially overestimated the degree of independence which they gained in 1956. After the initial jubilation over the increased Polish independence achieved at that time, there was, if anything, some apprehension among the population that things were more likely to get worse than better for Poland. For the moment, however, most people preferred not to think about the future.

5: FROM THE THAW TO THE PRESENT

Changes in the Environment

A number of important changes in the external environment have taken place since 1958, all of which have affected Poland's integration with the communist system. The growing rift between the Soviet Union on the one hand and China and Albania on the other, the acceptance of the unorthodox Cuban state into the communist fold, the independent economic course taken by Rumania after 1962, and the growing independence and diversity of the nonruling communist parties have all contributed to the further erosion of the political authority of the U.S.S.R. and the monolithic character of the communist system, allowing Poland still more freedom in both foreign and domestic policy and increasing her importance within the system as an ally of the Soviet Union. The further development of the European Common Market and the European Free Trade Area, the continued revitalization of the Council for Mutual Economic Assistance, and the beginnings of an East-West détente have all affected the course and nature of Polish economic integration with the communist world. Finally, the continually increasing importance of the Federal Republic of Germany and its diplomatic offensive in East Europe after 1966, the deterioration of the solidarity of the NATO alliance, French President DeGaulle's diplomatic maneuvering in Europe, and the Vietnam war have had an important impact on Poland's political orientation toward both the communist world and the West.

Changes in the Belief System

Although the difference between the official culture and the popular culture remained much smaller than it had been before 1956, most of the popular enthusiasm for the new government gradually diminished as the unifying excitement of the confrontation with the U.S.S.R. in October, 1956, faded away. It soon became clear to the Polish people that Gomulka was, indeed, really a dedicated communist, not a democrat in communist clothing as many had half-consciously and naively hoped. The reforms, however, had made life more tolerable, and it was easier to accept what was now clear to most Poles: Poland was going to be part of the communist world for a long time to come, both because of the threat of Soviet military action in the event of an uprising and because of the Western powers' inability and lack of willingness to intervene. Moreover, the increased economic and military strength of the Federal German Republic made the Poles more dependent than ever on the Soviet Union for the defense of their recovered territories.

The bulk of the Polish people continued to believe that extensive welfare measures, widespread public ownership of basic industries and communications facilities, and central planning were desirable, but they hoped to see these developed along the lines of a more pragmatic model. They still wanted more personal freedom and more independence in trade and foreign affairs. By the early 1960s, however, they had lost any real hope of achieving these goals and contented themselves with retreating into their own private and family lives, enjoying whatever satisfactions income, ingenuity, friends, and good fortune could provide.

Identification with the West—particularly with England, France, and the United States—probably increased during the early part of this period, but at the same time respect for the Soviet Union also developed because of its more liberal policies toward Poland and because of its growing technological achievements. The war in Vietnam also cost the United States considerable respect, particularly among the youth.

It is important to remember that by the end of 1964 Poland had already been under communist rule for 20 years. Well over one-third of the population had been born after the communists had taken power, and over half the people had received at least part of their education since then. A sizable percentage of the population, then, had experienced the economic and political systems of only the German occupation of World War II and the postwar communist rule. Living under communist rule, therefore, is rapidly becoming the normal rather than the abnormal state of affairs for the Polish population.

The communist elite has also long since come to view its rule as normal and permanent. Although the Polish communists believe that their own interests and those of the Polish nation require close association with the rest of the communist system to maintain a unified front against the noncommunist West, especially against a rearmed Germany, they remain domestically oriented and little interested in taking risks in support of communist expansion. They have strongly supported the Soviet Union against China and against

Poland's more extreme and orthodox neighbors, though they have also opposed an open split within the communist world.

Changes in the Social System

The Political Subsystem. Poland today remains undisputably controlled by the PZPR. Within the Party there is still a relatively great degree of Party democracy (compared with the pre-1956 period), but whatever really free discussion there was during the thaw has apparently been reduced to a minimum with power still clearly concentrated at the top levels of the Party. Though the Central Committee, Politburo, and Secretariat are not without influence in establishing policy, and despite some signs of quiet political ferment at the top levels of the PZPR since 1959, Gomulka seems to be ever more firmly in control of the Party and the all-important professional Party apparatus.[1] The number of people in top positions of the Party and government favoring a harder domestic policy—particularly in the economic sphere—seems to have been increasing in recent years, though it is difficult to assess how much this is a result of Gomulka's personal preference and how much of it is because of the political strength and organization of those elements in the PZPR leadership whose demands Gomulka has had to take into account.[2]

[1]In 1964 the professional apparatus numbered 7,180, including over 1,600 with at least some higher education, according to Zenon Kliszko, "Zmiany w Statucie PZPR i Niektore Problemy Polityczne-Organizacacyjne Partii," *IV Zjazd PZPR* (Warszawa: Ksiazka i Wiedza, 1964), p. 237.

[2]For some more detailed interpretations of recent developments in the PZPR see: Jerzy Ptakowski, "Politics in Poland," *East Europe,* 11 (Dec., 1962) 18–25; "Political Maneuvers in

Between 1957 and 1959 a series of minor purges removed extremists and unproductive opportunists from both the revisionist and Stalinist factions of the Party. By 1959, when the Third Party Congress was held, Gomulka had fully consolidated his position in the PZPR and had directed the Party back to its primary task of making Poland a socialist state—but at a moderate speed and with proper allowances for Polish tradition and needs. Between 1959 and 1964, when the Fourth Party Congress eventually convened, another 210,000 full and candidate members were dropped from the PZPR lists or expelled, and over 800,000 more were recruited in the Party's continual and often frustrated efforts to build a strong, faithful, and dedicated Party membership.[3]

The secret police system has gradually increased in size and scope since the relative moderation of the 1956–57 period. Most of its efforts, however, have been in the combatting of economic crimes against the state-owned system of production and distribution. Political surveillance, however, is also apparently on the increase. The few formal attempts at protest over the direction of developments in Poland have had little success and have often led to reprisals—for example, the case of the 34 intellectuals who protested the lack of freedom of expression in 1964, the subsequent trial of author Melchoir Wankowicz,[4] and the case of

---

Warsaw," *East Europe,* 13 (April, 1964); and R. F. Staar, "Warsaw's Quiet Congress," *East Europe,* 13 (Aug., 1964) 2–6.

[3] Note that the number of new members taken in between 1959 and 1964 was over half of the not quite 1,600,000 total full and candidate membership of the PZPR in June, 1964. See: Zenon Kliszko, "Zmiany w Statucie PZPR," pp. 235–41.

[4] For details see: Gaston de Cerezay, "Gomulka and the Intellectuals," *East Europe,* 13 (Dec., 1964), 22–30.

Kuron and Modzelewski.[5] The student demonstrations of February and March 1968 also met with strong repressive action by the Party and triggered off a significant number of purges of high-ranking government and Party officials. The sweeping liberal changes which took place in Czechoslovakia in late 1967 and early 1968 will undoubtedly affect developments in Poland but it is too early to tell just what impact they will have.

Despite the greater formalization of CMEA and the formation of numerous multilateral committees and organizations for interstate co-operation, there continues to be a significant difference in kind of political integration which has been the rule since 1956. First, the U.S.S.R. had ceased to be the sole organizer and director of the relationships between the communist-ruled states. There has been much wider contact, consultation, and co-operation between Poland and the other communist-ruled states of eastern Europe. In short, the integration is now truly multilateral, diffuse, and decentralized, rather than bilateral, highly centralized, and controlled by the U.S.S.R. Second, the contacts and co-operation have not been limited exclusively to the member states of the communist system. There has been more tolerance of co-operation with both the deviant communist-ruled states such as Yugoslavia and with the noncommunist states of the West and the less developed areas of the world. Third, the Soviet exercise of control is much more limited than before, and much more attention has been paid to Polish demands and interests. The consultation process, although still under ultimate Soviet control, is much more a two-way affair. The Polish government and

[5]For details see: Alexander Bregman, "The Strange Case of Kuron and Modzelewski," *East Europe*, 15 (Dec., 1966), 7–11.

Party leaders—like the leaders of the other member states of the system—have had much more latitude for making independent decisions in domestic policy. In fact, this independence has probably increased because of Soviet recognition of the inadequacy of the Stalinist model of socialist society, the Sino–Soviet dispute, and the general deterioration of the solidarity of the communist system.

It is interesting to note that in recent years the degree of substantive co-operation between Poland and the U.S.S.R. has probably increased—at least in foreign affairs—as a result of the coincidence of Polish and Soviet interests following the Sino–Soviet rift and the rearmament of West Germany. Consultative meetings between the Polish and Soviet leaders have been especially frequent since the fall of Khrushchev.[6] The Poles seem to have been working particularly hard to strengthen the ties between Poland, the U.S.S.R., Czechoslovakia, and the G.D.R. as a bulwark against a rearmed German Federal Republic.[7]

There are also some signs that Poland has played more than a passive role in the sphere of foreign policy. Poland has pressed for a moderate, system-wide

[6]In addition to numerous meetings between Soviet and Polish Party and government officials at multilateral political and economic gatherings, Gomulka and Brezhnev met privately for consultation at least four times in the course of the year following their first meeting in October, 1964—once in January, 1965, and again in April, September, and late October, 1965.

[7]See: "Poland's Plan for the 'Northern Tier'," *East Europe,* 15 (Nov., 1966), 9–16. Poland also signed new twenty-year treaties of friendship, co-operation, and mutual assistance, with Czechoslovakia (March 1, 1967), the G.D.R. (March 15, 1967), and Bulgaria (April 6, 1967) as part of a co-ordinated campaign to provide support for the G.D.R. and to offset the U.S. and West German campaign to isolate the G.D.R.

foreign policy in relation to the capitalist world, but has been reluctant to agree with Soviet plans for a multilateral Party meeting to deal with the Sino–Soviet dispute. Although the PZPR has been willing to acknowledge the leading position of the U.S.S.R. in the communist system, the Polish Party leaders have continued to emphasize the sovereignty of each individual state and communist party and have not been willing to accept the idea that either the U.S.S.R. or any multilateral Party conference has the authority to make binding decisions for individual states, especially in domestic affairs.

Poland has been allowed the prestige of presenting its own foreign policy proposals to the West, for example, the Rapacki plan for a nuclear free zone in central Europe and, more recently, the Gomulka plan for a freeze on nuclear weapons in central Europe. The Poles have also played an active part in the recent détente with western Europe, most notably with France, Italy, and Austria, between 1965 and 1967.[8] Relations with the Federal Republic of Germany have remained cool because of the Oder-Neisse boundary

[8]Poland in July, 1965, concluded a far-reaching agreement with Italy on economic, technical, and industrial co-operation—the first such agreement between Poland and a state outside the communist system—and in October Italian President Saragat paid a state visit to Poland. The following year a $40,000,000 agreement was signed for the production of Fiat automobiles in Poland under a licensing agreement. In September, 1965, Polish Premier Cyrankiewicz paid highly publicized state visits to France and Austria, and in October a five year Polish-French trade agreement was signed calling for much-expanded trade and other forms of co-operation. The following January, France lifted quotas and tariffs on 670 manufactured items for export to eastern Europe. Finally, in 1967, Polish Foreign Minister Rapacki paid a visit to France, followed by a one-week visit to Poland by President de Gaulle in September.

question and the West German government's attempts to isolate the G.D.R. from Poland and the rest of the communist world. Nevertheless, a permanent West German trade mission was allowed to establish itself in Warsaw in 1963, and economic co-operation agreements were concluded with several West German firms after 1965. At the same time, Poland has been one of the most active east European states in its denunciation of the United States for involvement in the war in Vietnam, thereby weakening the friendly ties with the U.S. which developed during the earlier part of this period.

The Military Subsystem. There has been no extensive change apparent in the Polish military except for the modernization of weapons. Its officers remain almost entirely Polish. Poland still continues to take an active part in the Warsaw Pact and voluntarily integrates its forces with those of the rest of the members. How reliable the Polish armed forces would be in the event of a major war with the West is an open question, but it is clear that they would fight to protect their recovered territories or if they were faced by German armies.

The Economic Subsystem.[9] A number of important economic changes have been introduced since 1957. Although there has been no resumption of the collec-

---

[9]See: J. M. Montias, "The Polish Economic Model," *Problems of Communism,* 9 (March–April, 1960); J. M. Montias and Alfred Zauberman, "The Polish Economy, 1961," *Survey* (Jan.–March, 1961), pp. 50–60; Michael Gamarnikow, "Wages and the State," *East Europe,* 12 (July, 1963), 2–5; and "Poland's Economic Recession," *East Europe,* 12 (March, 1963), 13–18.

tivization drive, there has been an extensive campaign to introduce the "agricultural circle" as a substitute for the collective farm. The agricultural circle, which is in many ways similar to the prewar co-operatives of the Polish Peasant Party (PSL), functions as an agricultural extension service, co-operative tractor and machinery rental agency, agricultural supply center, and also as a stimulus to co-operation and modernization.[10] Although the agricultural circles have had considerable success in boosting production, they have not solved the basic problems of the surplus of people on the land, the fundamentally subsistence nature of Polish agriculture,[11] and the continual shortage of fertilizer and fodder. Moreover, because of the high prices the government has paid the peasant to stimulate production, the peasants have become the wealthiest major group in Poland, despite the increases in land taxes introduced to combat this tendency.[12]

[10]The circles are financed in large part by government funds earned from the difference between the open market price and the price the government pays for the compulsory deliveries.

[11]The table below provides a good picture of the relative size of the private agricultural land holdings in 1960 (accounting for over 85 per cent of the arable land in Poland):

Size of land holding in hectares	% of individual farms	% of arable land (in individual farms)
0.1– 0.5	9.6	0.5
0.5– 2.0	23.0	5.8
2.0– 5.0	30.5	21.7
5.0–10.0	26.2	39.4
10.0–20.0	9.7	32.6
20.0 & above	1.0	32.6

Maly Rocznik Statystyczny, 1963, p. 117.

[12]In late 1963 an "agrominimum" program was decreed by the Council of Ministers (*Monitor Polski*, no. 85). It consists

The Polish system of private agriculture[13] has been a source of friction between Poland and its eastern European neighbors, who were pushing hard for and achieving complete collectivization of their own peasants. Interestingly enough, however, it has received some guarded praise from top Soviet officials since 1961 and seems to have been fully accepted by the CPSU, at least for the time being.

In industry more attention continues to be paid to the production of consumer's goods and items for foreign trade in an attempt to overcome Poland's chronic balance of payments deficit. Private enterprise is still tolerated and even encouraged if an item is considered important by the state and is produced in insufficient quantities by the socialized sectors of the economy. Government controls, high taxes, and uncertainty

---

of eight rules to be followed by all private farmers (providing the local government organ in the area agrees) to insure the most productive use of their land. The rules, in short, require the peasants to (1) cultivate all usable land, (2) rotate crops, (3) carry out post-harvest grain skimming and prewinter plowing, (4) lime the fields, (5) use mechanical seeding, (6) use mineral fertilizer and farmyard manure, (7) follow conservation measures on meadows and pastures and harvest according to local schedules, (8) use proper hygiene in the care of livestock.

In early 1968 a new Party program for further rationalization of agriculture was passed by the Sejm. It provided for consolidation of small privately-owned plots of land by local government councils; public auctioning of land "not rationally" used by the owner; and lifelong pensions and a hectar of land to use for peasants who voluntarily transfer their farm land to the state, though retaining ownership of their buildings.

[13]In 1963, 85.7 per cent of the arable land was in individual farms (accounting for 89 per cent of total production), 1.6 per cent of the land was in collective farms (1.2 per cent of total production), and 12.7 per cent of the land was in state farms (9.8 per cent of total production). *Maly Rocznik Statystyczny, 1963,* p. 115.

about the future, however, have kept the private sector from growing.[14]

At the same time investment has continued at a high level. The economy continued to grow rapidly until 1962–63 when bad weather, poor harvests, and a host of economic problems caused a considerable slowdown in the rate of growth.[15] This economic crisis was followed by sharp increases in the price of fuel and certain basic foods in 1963. Though the variety and quantity of consumer goods available has increased appreciably since 1957, there has been only a relatively slow increase in real wages for most urban dwellers, and after 1963 a rise in prices resulted in a temporary decrease in real wages for many Poles. Nevertheless, there has been a steady, if slow, increase in the living standard in Poland throughout this period.

Government has maintained control over production. The short 1956–57 experiment with workers' councils ended quickly when PZPR policy called for their absorption into communist-controlled factory "workers' self-government conferences," which had representatives from management, the workers' councils (if they existed in the plant), the labor unions,

[14]In fact, between 1960 and 1962 private production and the total sales in private shops decreased somewhat though they have remained at a constant level since then. See: *Maly Rocznik Statystyczny, 1967,* pp. 64, 159.

[15]In 1964, however, the economy on the whole apparently performed more satisfactorily. See *Zycie Gospodarcze* (Oct. 4, 1964), p. 10. The rate of industrial growth for these years (rounded off to the nearest per cent) is as follows, according to Polish sources: 1961, 10 per cent; 1962, 8 per cent; 1963, 5 per cent; 1964, 9 per cent; 1965, 9 per cent; 1966, 7 per cent. *Maly Rocznik Statystyczny, 1967,* pp. 62–63. [See Table 8 in the Appendix for additional data.]

and the local Party cells. In the past three or four years there has also been a noticeable tendency to appoint former Stalinist officials to positions of importance in the Party and government economic-planning apparatus. After the recent economic crisis there seems to have been growing sympathy in Party circles for tightening the control over the economy, increasing labor discipline, and pushing harder for economic development.

Perhaps the most important economic change in this period was the revitalization of CMEA. A formal charter was drawn up in 1959 and signed the following year. In 1962 an Executive Committee was established to provide decision-making authority at the highest level. CMEA, with apparent Polish support, continued its attempt to co-ordinate the economic development plans of its member states, aiming at the development of a more rational division of labor in the communist world. Numerous difficulties arose, however, in the course of working out the specialization agreements, and by 1964 the Poles began to show signs of dissatisfaction with CMEA and to use more caution in statements about the organization, emphasizing its advisory role and the sovereignty of the member states. Nevertheless, considerable progress has clearly been made in assigning production specializations.[16]

In 1962, for example, Poland and Hungary formed the Haldex Corporation to exploit Hungarian coal slack—the first such international joint-enterprise

[16]Between the middle of 1962 and the end of 1965, for example, CMEA adopted specialization recommendations on 900 varieties of machinery alone, with Poland allocated 250. See: Piotr Jaroszewicz, "For Development of International Ties of the Polish Economy," *Polish Perspectives,* 9 (Nov., 1966), 5.

agreement in the communist world. Poland and five other CMEA countries established a Bearing Industry Co-operation Organization to co-ordinate specialization in this area. In addition, Poland, Czechoslovakia, and Hungary in 1964 formed "Intermetal" to facilitate co-operation in iron and steel production; they were later joined by the U.S.S.R., Bulgaria, and the G.D.R. (Additional agreements have been worked out among the CMEA members for sharing the investment burden of the states that are called upon to develop mines or industry that require a heavy capital outlay and are intended primarily to serve the raw-material needs of other states.)

Other agreements were reached to facilitate co-operation and co-ordination as well as specialization. In this period CMEA continued its attempt to promote trade within the communist world by developing machinery for alleviating the balance-of-payments problem between the member states. The Bank for Economic Co-operation was finally set up in 1964 to provide a multilateral clearing house for CMEA. It has not proven completely satisfactory and has only partially acquiesced in the Poles' request that more of the Bank's capital be in gold and convertible currency to further facilitate CMEA trade. CMEA has also tried—but again with inconclusive results—to facilitate trade and make specialization more rational by working on a scheme for comparative analysis of costs and prices in the various member states.[17] An Institute for Standardization was established in Moscow in 1962. In the same year Poland completed the integration of her power grid with those of her neighbors through the Central Power Distribution System. The Friendship

[17]For details see Kaser, *COMECON,* pp. 128–30.

Pipeline—linking Poland, Czechoslovakia, and the G.D.R. with the Soviet oilfields—was constructed in this period. A Joint Freight Car Pool was also set up in mid-1964. There has been continued success in the areas of technical co-operation, contacts between specialists,[18] and the co-ordination of research efforts with exchanges of documentation, licenses, and training fellowships, particularly in the areas of industry, agriculture, and health. Poland has taken an active part in the International Nuclear Research Institute in Dubna (in the U.S.S.R.). Also of interest is the fact that in April, 1967, Poland sent a delegation of experts to Moscow to meet with representatives from other communist-ruled states to discuss space co-operation.[19]

One of the major reasons for the above developments has been the desire to increase further the overall trade turnover among the CMEA members, to increase their economic interdependence, and to develop their collective economic self-sufficiency. This goal of increased trade turnover has been reached, both with respect to the absolute level of trade and to the proportion of the members' trade with each other. In 1965, for example, nearly 60 per cent of Poland's foreign trade was with the other CMEA members, and another 4 per cent of it with other communist-ruled states. [See Table 5 in the Appendix.]

The proportion of Polish trade with the noncommunist states continued at a high level during this period, but it declined from the peak of 41.6 per cent of total Polish trade turnover reached in 1958 to a low of around 35 per cent in 1963. The 1966 figure was

[18]For details see Kaser, *COMECON*.

[19]The conference included experts from Bulgaria, Czechoslovakia, Cuba, Mongolia, the G.D.R., Poland, Rumania, and the U.S.S.R. *Trybuna Ludu*, April 16, 1967.

119

about 37 per cent, including 35.7 per cent of Polish imports and 38.4 per cent of her exports. [See Table 3 in the Appendix.] The Soviet share of Polish trade had declined to a low of just over 26 per cent in 1958, but thereafter climbed steadily to a high of just over 33 per cent in 1965 and 32.2 per cent in 1966. [See Table 4 in the Appendix.] Czechoslovakia, the G.D.R., and Great Britain continued to be Poland's next most important trading partners, followed by the U.S., Hungary, Yugoslavia, West Germany, Italy, and France.[20] [See Table 5 in the Appendix.] After 1959 there was also a significant increase in credit-financed trade with the underdeveloped countries.

Poland still remained largely dependent on the U.S.S.R. for essential imports of petroleum and iron and manganese ores. Most machinery imports came from the U.S.S.R., Czechoslovakia, and the G.D.R. The United States, however, became the chief supplier of grain and fats and a very important source of cotton (37 per cent in 1958; about 20 per cent in 1965), although for reasons discussed below Polish agricultural imports from the U.S. declined significantly after 1964. [See Table 6 in the Appendix.]

The United States became the chief source of economic aid for Poland during the first part of this period by providing on a yearly basis large quantities of surplus agricultural commodities which the Poles could purchase under very favorable terms on long-term credit.[21] After 1964, however, Congress limited Poland to five-year credit in the purchase of surplus agricultural commodities and such favorable terms were no longer available. Nevertheless, between 1957

[20]Note that the order of importance of these trading partners varies from year to year.

[21]*Rocznik Statystyczny, 1959,* pp. 255–57.

and 1964 Poland received well over half a billion dollars worth of U.S. surplus agricultural commodities on long-term credit.[22]

It is worth noting that since 1964 Poland has been putting more emphasis on the importance of expanding trade with the West as well as with the communist world. There has been continuing concern over preserving old markets in western Europe and bridging the tariff walls of the EEC and EFTA to provide an outlet for new exports. In March, 1965, the Poles discussed farm exports with the EEC Executive Committee in Brussels, and in April, 1966, a Polish delegation held even more far-reaching—though apparently inconclusive—talks with the EEC.[23] The Poles and the Czechs also participated in the Kennedy round of tariff negotiations. Finally in 1966, after a decade of loose association with GATT, Poland became a full member of the organization. In addition, Poland has been doing a great deal since 1965 to explore expanded trade opportunities with the West on a bilateral basis. In late 1965 the first U.S. commercial trade

[22]Between 1957 and 1964 about $600,000,000 worth of surplus agricultural commodities were sold to Poland under the provisions of Title I of PL 480, which allowed Poland to make a zloty deposit equaling the amount of the sale in a U.S. account in Poland; by mutual consent of the U.S. and Polish governments in Poland, after twenty years the zloty that had not been used were, in theory anyway, to be repaid to the U.S. in dollars without interest. Since 1963, however, some sales have also been made under the provisions of Title IV, which in the case of Poland, provides for five-year credits repayable in dollars with interest. In 1964 Congress eliminated any further sales to Poland under the more generous Title I provisions. For Polish reaction, see: W. Wirski, "To Nie Jest Komercjalizacja," *Polityka* (Nov. 8, 1964), p. 1.

[23]Delegations from Czechoslovakia, Yugoslavia, and Rumania participated in informal talks with the EEC at the same time.

missions since the war were sent to Poland and Rumania.[24]

Poland has also shown considerable interest since 1964 in exploring new forms of co-operation with individual Western firms. A number of agreements providing various forms of joint manufacturing and distribution operations were signed with Western firms. In 1965, for example, the Polish government and IBAG, a West German firm, signed an agreement providing joint ownership of a company to handle Polish machinery imports and exports, making use of the German firm's distribution facilities in the West. In 1966 a 40 million dollar agreement was reached with Fiat of Italy for the manufacture of automobiles in Poland under a licensing arrangement.

Although Poland is no longer as completely dependent on the communist world for as many imports and export markets as in the Stalinist period, most of the dependency remains, giving the U.S.S.R. considerable leverage in dealing with Poland. Both in making trade agreements and in the determination of specialization Poland has retained a good measure of veto power, though by exerting enough pressure the U.S.S.R. can usually force an issue if its demands are not too much opposed to Polish economic interests.

The Communications Subsystem. Communications within Poland remained much freer, less centralized, and less one-way than before 1955, and the Poles still felt free to criticize and express themselves in unorthodox ways, despite the tightening of the censorship. Although the Party-controlled press has taken a position closer to that of the Soviet Union on all major foreign-policy issues, particularly after 1961, compared

[24]*New York Times,* Sept. 14, 1965.

with the Soviet press there has remained a remarkable amount of objectivity in the reporting of events. Since 1961–62 there has also been a tightening of censorship and considerably more pressure put on the artists and writers to help spread socialist attitudes and values. Nevertheless, they have retained a wide range of freedom to experiment with new methods and ideas, if not to criticize socialism or the Soviet Union.

The volume of communications with states outside the communist system continued to rise, increasing the frequency of Polish contact with Western cultural ideas. Cultural agreements were signed with a number of Western states, including France and the United States. One of the agreements with the United States created a media-guarantee program that enabled Poland to purchase American films, books, newspapers, and magazines with Polish currency.[25] Foreign-student exchanges with the West also greatly increased in the early part of this period, as did other exchange programs, though increased international tensions have caused a leveling off in such exchanges, particularly with the United States.[26] Western books, magazines, and newspapers have been available on a limited basis in Poland throughout this period, and a high proportion of the full-length feature films shown in the

[25]Under the provisions of this agreement the Poles purchased a large number of American films and imported among other items the *New York Times, Newsweek,* and tens of thousands of books each year for sale in Poland. In 1967 Congress cut back the funds for such programs and the future of the program in Poland is in doubt.

[26]In addition to exchange programs, large numbers of Poles have come to the U.S. each year on various private and public fellowships and travel grants. The Ford and Rockefeller programs and the Department of State foreign visitor programs have been particularly significant in this regard.

123

cinema are from the West.[27] There is also a significant exchange of musicians, artists, and theater groups under the provisions of the cultural exchange programs Poland has with 80 countries. In 1966, for example, 5,000 Polish cultural emissaries went abroad —100 music and theater ensembles, 362 art exhibitions, and 224 films. In return 80 foreign music ensembles, 186 art exhibitions, and 291 foreign films came to Poland.[28] Polish scientists are also active abroad and participate in 140 international scientific, technical, and economic organizations.[29] There is also an annual book fair in Warsaw every spring; in 1966 nearly 200 foreign publishers brought displays.

Travel to and from Poland continued to increase in this period in relation both to the West and to the other communist-ruled states of eastern Europe.[30]

[27]In 1963, for example, the full-length films shown in Poland included 27 Polish, 37 Soviet, 21 British, 17 French, and 15 American films. *PAP*, Jan. 11, 1964.

[28]*Nowe Drogi,* July, 1966.

[29]See: *Polish Perspectives,* 9 (Nov., 1966), 7.

[30]The following table provides some recent statistics (in thousands) on travel to and from Poland:

To Poland	1956	1961	1962	1963	1964
Member states of the communist system	64.1	202.2	350.1	220.7	358.8
Nonmember states	14.0	50.6	55.3	64.5	92.2

From Poland		1961	1962	1963	
Member states of the communist system		328.2	395.3	332.0	
Nonmember states		43.6	51.0	53.6	

Adapted from: Dariusz Fikus, "Podroze," *Polityka* (Jan. 9, 1965), p. 9. [See also, Table 9 in the Appendix.]

There has been a particularly significant mushrooming of tourist travel between Poland and the other CMEA states in the last few years because of recent easing of visa restrictions. Early in this period a limited convention with Czechoslovakia was signed, providing easy access to resort areas along the border of the two countries without need for a passport. Since 1965 additional agreements have been made with the U.S.S.R., Czechoslovakia, and Bulgaria, further easing travel restrictions. In 1965, for example, Bulgaria and Poland signed an agreement abolishing the need for visas by citizens of the other state. The volume of mail and telephone calls to and from Poland also continued to grow rapidly throughout this period. [See Table 11 in the Appendix.]

Another important development in this period has been the establishment of Intervision, the east European TV network linking Poland, Czechoslovakia, the U.S.S.R., the G.D.R., Hungary, Bulgaria, and Rumania. In addition to programs originating in these countries, there are occasional hookups with Eurovision, the western European TV network, and there have even been a number of transmissions from the United States via satellite. There has also been a significant increase in the number of TV receivers in Poland in this period—from less than 85 thousand in 1958 to over 2.5 million in 1966.[31]

The Socialization Subsystem. Though socialism and socialist values are still heavily stressed in school, in the press, and through places of work, in general teaching and propaganda have remained much less dogmatic and much more objective than before 1956.

---

[31]*Rocznik Statystyczny, 1959*, p. 310; *Maly Rocznik Statystyczny, 1967*, p. 209.

The young are generally taught to be critical, though not about socialism, the Soviet Union, or their own government's policies.

Censorship was tightened and pressure put on the writers and artists to spread socialist values and help build a socialist Poland. Although there still remained much more creative freedom than previously, after 1957 it was increasingly difficult to publish material or stage plays that were in any way critical of socialism, the Party, or the U.S.S.R.—even in satirical form.[32] Similarly, the discussion clubs that sprang up in 1955 and 1956 were all gradually shut down.[33] Party control of the press has also become increasingly close, with more and more specific directives coming from the Party Central Committee.

In 1958 the Party resumed its policy of weakening the role of the church in national affairs and began working to eliminate all remaining church functions in the fields of education, relief, hospital care, orphanages, and so forth. Religious classes continued to be taught in the schools until the 1959–62 period when an extensive campaign was launched to eliminate them. Though religious classes are still being held outside the schools, the government is putting pressure on the churches to abandon them by restricting who can teach and where classes can be held. Higher taxes have been imposed on the church, and more recently the state has attempted to increase its control over instruction in the seminaries. The church has also faced increasing difficulty in obtaining permission to hold religious processions and has been refused per-

[32]See also: L. Labedz, "The Polish Intellectual Climate," *Survey* (Jan.–March, 1961), pp. 3–11.

[33]See Witold Jedlicki, "The Death of the Crooked Circle Club," *East Europe*, 12 (Aug., 1963), 10–13.

mission to build new churches. The summer of 1966 was a period of particularly intensive conflict between the Party and the church as both competed for the attention of the public during the Millennium celebrations. The government did its best to put obstacles in the way of the celebrations by the church, denied permission for the Pope and church officials from abroad to visit Poland for the event, and restricted the flow of Western tourists. Normal church services, however, have not been affected, the church still remains the major organization in Poland not under complete Party control, and the handful of Catholic deputies still have their seats in the Sejm. The church's influence among the youth, however, seems to be definitely on the wane.

The Degree of Integration: Its Costs and Benefits

Most of the costs of integration in this period resulted from the division of economic labor within the communist system. Poland was called upon to make heavy investments toward the exploitation of its mineral deposits, even though there were many more pressing investment needs that would have paid off much sooner. Poland did receive some investment help from the states that stood to benefit most—namely, the U.S.S.R., Czechoslovakia, and the G.D.R. —but it still had to bear a considerable burden. In addition, Poland's share of investment in its section of the Danube-Oder Canal will be of primary benefit to Czechoslovakia and the G.D.R. On the other hand, Poland benefited from joint mineral exploitation investment projects undertaken in some of the other communist states, most notably in the U.S.S.R.

Despite the fact that Poland was in many ways

growing more dependent on the other states of the communist world, the costs of integration were probably decreased as a result of its greater economic bargaining position within the system which resulted from its own increased national unity, greater trade with the noncommunist states, and the growing assertions of independence by other members of the communist system.[34] The relative advantage of trading with the West also decreased, however, as the Western prices for Polish exports fell, as those for imports from the West continued to rise, and as tariff barriers, keener competition from west European and American firms, and demands for increasingly higher quality products made markets outside the communist world harder to win.

It is also worth remembering that the perception of the earlier high costs of integration with the U.S.S.R. was fading rapidly. Although memories of the past caused many Poles to overexaggerate the current costs of integration with the communist system, most Poles in this period directed their major complaints at the domestic communist regime and its economic policies.

Most Polish communists were probably reasonably satisfied with the existing state of integration in this period, save in economic matters where there were some reservations about Poland's assignments in the economic division of labor in the system. A large majority of the politically active Polish population, however, still felt that there was too much integration with the Soviet Union and the communist system and too little with the West, particularly after Rumania's success in turning to the West for greater trade bene-

[34]But see also: Aleksander Kutt, "Exploitation in Soviet Bloc Trade," *East Europe,* 11 (May, 1962), 21–24.

fits. Even the general Polish population, however, was beginning to recognize the importance of Soviet cooperation in protecting the recovered territories, though most people had not changed their basic desire to see Poland escape from the communist system and to effect basic changes in their domestic socioeconomic system.

The experience of the past few years had proven to the Poles that even if they could not change the pattern of integration completely to their liking, they could at least effect a tolerable compromise if the Polish communist elite felt it was important. Therefore, although there was some expectation of closer economic integration with the communist system and some expectation that it would be more costly than similar integration with the West, there was a general belief that the costs could be kept reasonably low. Because of the increased independence being shown by the other communist-ruled states, there was some expectation on the part of the intellectuals that the Polish bargaining position vis-à-vis the system might even increase with time, thereby making Poland more independent. The more educated Poles also felt there was a good possibility of increasing trade with the West. These expectations of change, however, were not widespread among the population. Most people simply accepted the existing state of integration as inevitable and thought little about any possible future change.

6: SUMMARY AND CONCLUSION

Before World War II Poland was largely independent and not well integrated with any other single state or system. Least of all was Poland integrated with the states that now form the communist party state system. The closest political integration was with France and the closest economic integration was with Great Britain, Germany, and the United States.

At the end of World War II Poland entered the communist system as the Red Army and the Soviet secret police supported a Soviet-sponsored and communist-dominated Polish coalition government that gradually infiltrated and controlled all Polish institutions except the Roman Catholic church. The government was controlled largely by the Soviet Union, which allowed the Poles to make no decisions contrary to Soviet interests and which forced the Polish government to agree to many decisions that were clearly opposed to the interests of the Polish communist elite and the population as a whole.

After the Polish communists had consolidated their position, the U.S.S.R. used its influence to mold Polish society and government even more according to the Soviet model. There were few formal instruments of integration, but co-ordination with the U.S.S.R.

and the rest of the communist system was achieved through informal channels of control: Soviet demands were communicated through contacts between the CPSU and the PPR (later the PZPR), the Polish and Soviet Embassies, the Party press, and Soviet agents holding positions in Poland. The information-gathering system provided by the secret police, the Soviet Embassy, and Soviet agents in Polish positions kept the U.S.S.R. informed about whether or not its demands were being carried out. The ultimate threat of Soviet intervention by force and the resulting Soviet veto over choices of personnel for key posts insured that the Polish leaders would carry out Soviet demands.

The Polish communist elite were further tied to the Soviet Union by their own dependence on the U.S.S.R. for their continued exercise of power and for protection against Western anticommunist intervention. All the Poles were increasingly dependent on the U.S.S.R. for protection of their recovered territories from German attempts to reconquer them.

Economic development progressed in Poland (at the direction of the Soviet Union) in such a way that the Polish economy was to a large extent built around specialized plants that required Soviet raw materials and that produced goods for special Soviet needs, thereby increasing Polish dependence upon the U.S.S.R. In addition, the proportion of Polish trade with the U.S.S.R. and the rest of the communist-ruled states was very high, increasing steadily from 1948 to 1954 when it began to decline. Many aspects of these economic relations with the U.S.S.R. were very costly to Poland, particularly before 1956.

Poland, in short, became integrated into the communist system largely by force with the help of a small minority of Polish supporters who were either willing to accept the loss of Polish sovereignty as the price for holding power and seeing Poland transformed into a Soviet-style socialist state, or who saw this loss of sovereignty as inevitable and thought the best course of action was collaboration with the U.S.S.R. in hope of salvaging something for Poland in the process. Since most Poles who helped set up the new regime were also Polish nationalists, considerable resentment developed concerning Soviet control over Poland and the economic costs that this type of integration with the communist world had brought. Most of the Polish population, however, opposed not only the economic costs of integration and the loss of independence for the Polish state, but also the indirect political and social costs of an unwanted government and unwanted social changes.

It was not until 1956 that the nationalistically oriented Polish elite were able to unite and take advantage of Soviet weakness to win more independence for Poland—especially in domestic policy—and to decrease the economic and psychological costs of integration. At the same time, the Polish elite were forced to make concessions to the population to make communist rule more palatable.

Though most Poles were less than enthusiastic about communist rule, they became increasingly resigned to it except for the brief period in 1956 when there was some popular hope that Poland might escape it. Tight control by the Polish communists and the threat of ultimate Soviet military intervention made the possibility of a successful revolution seem very remote, particularly after the failure of the Hungarian uprising. After 1956, however, as a result of the newly acquired power of the Polish communists to exercise more influence on Soviet and system-wide decisions affecting Poland, and because of the disappearance of the ostensible signs of Soviet control, the degree of consensus over integration increased considerably both within the Polish communist elite and among the Polish population.

At the same time the more favorable Polish bargaining position vis-à-vis the U.S.S.R., the abandonment of the Stalinist model of autarky for the smaller communist-ruled states, and increased contacts at all levels between the Party and government officials of the eastern European states led to the possibility of a qualitatively different kind of integration in eastern Europe—one based much more on the mutual advantage of the individual partners. The result was a lower–level integration, less centralization of decision–making authority, more difficulties in reaching agreement, and a narrower range of activities successfully co-ordinated, but far more consensus over the results. Moreover, there have been enough potentially profitable areas of co-operation to bring about a mushrooming of multilateral conferences, committees, and organizations both inside and outside the framework of CMEA, and a substantial reinforcement of the economic and political interdependency. The Polish elite has had the privilege of playing a major role in laying the groundwork for this new approach to integration.

Given an opportunity to leave the communist system, most of the Polish population would undoubtedly agree to do so, providing that it could be done peacefully, that Polish economic needs could be met elsewhere, that Poland would not lose its recovered territories, and that it would not be achieved at the cost of control by some other state or alien system. They would also want to retain a basically socialist society in preference to a return to the prewar system. Politically, they would probably be content with a system such as that of France under De Gaulle.

The Polish elite, on the other hand, would certainly hesitate to leave the system, and would hardly agree to do so unless they were certain that there would be no outside anticommunist interference and that they could maintain control over the Polish population. Even then, however, a good share of the elite would undoubtedly refuse to do so for ideological reasons as long as Poland remained reasonably autonomous within the system, as long as no intolerable demands were made, and as long as the current economic costs of integration remained as low as they are at present. Unless near-total immobilization of Soviet military power in Europe were to occur and the West were to intervene, it is doubtful that the general population could bring about Poland's exit from the communist system without the support of at least a good portion of the communist elite.

Even if political circumstances should make this possible, the changes that have taken place in Poland during the first 20 years of communist rule have created considerable practical obstacles to Poland's exit from the system. First, a great deal of investment has been devoted to industries and equipment that are designed either to use raw materials or spare parts from other communist states or to produce products specifically for export to those states. Conversion, although not impossible, would be expensive. Second, it would not now be easy for Poland to capture alternative markets because of the substandard quality of so many Polish products and the relatively low level of economic and technological development in relation to the needs of the West. Third, the highly advanced

135

and efficient level of industry in western Europe, keen competition between the various western European and American firms, the increasing degree of economic integration in western Europe, and Western tariffs and quotas on Polish imports present additional obstacles to the sale of Polish goods outside the communist world.

In addition, twenty years of communist rule have brought subtle but significant changes in the political outlook of the population at large, especially of the growing technical, bureaucratic, and intellectual cadres that have been co-opted into the ruling political structure of People's Poland. These changes in outlook have increased the political and cultural differences between the Poles and the peoples of the West, thereby increasing the difficulties of any potential integration with the states of western Europe.

Poland, in short, has had its alternatives restricted as the price of more than twenty years of communist rule and planned integration into the communist system. Poland was unable to take advantage of postwar opportunities for sales of coal in the West, was not allowed to benefit from the Marshall Plan aid, and could not make use of the licensing and investment resources of Western firms. It did not share fully in the benefits of German reparations payments, had to share the cost of Soviet troops stationed on Polish soil and of the transportation of goods and troops between Germany and the U.S.S.R., and was forced to pay the economic price of the cold war and rearmament. It furthermore was burdened with both the waste and mistakes of the Stalinist-imposed economic system and the discrimination against skilled managers and leaders who were considered politically unreliable, had to pay the cost of price discrimination in trade with the

Soviet Union, had its trade alternatives limited even more by agreeing to specialize to meet the needs of the other CMEA members, and was generally hampered by political dogmatism that severely restricted the decision-making freedom of the Polish economists and planners and effectively cut Poland off from the technical knowledge and skills of the West.

Although it seems most unlikely that Poland will overcome the political and economic obstacles in the way of completely leaving the communist system, there is still a good possibility that Poland—even under the leadership of the PZPR—will gradually increase its trade and economic co-operation with the West and move toward a position in which it maintains considerable economic and political integration with the system, but at the same time is more closely integrated economically (and even to some extent politically) with the West and the less developed countries of Asia, Latin America, and Africa. Whether this takes place will depend not only on Polish efforts to win Western markets and improve political relations with the Western states, but also on whether the West encourages co-operation in hopes of strengthening those forces in Poland which favor more friendly ties with the West and more liberal and pragmatic policies at home. Good possibilities also exist for the West to influence Poland's social, cultural, and communication integration as a result of the Poles' traditional ties with western Europe and the United States.

Even though any changes in Poland's political and military organization depend primarily on what happens in Poland, in the PZPR, and in the other states of the communist system, developments in the West and the policies of the Western governments are also of considerable importance. Western policies toward

137

Germany, the Polish-German frontier, and disarmament in central Europe and Vietnam are of particular significance in this respect. The general deterioration in the unity of the communist world over the past decade has made the policies of the Western states more crucial determinants of the direction and extent of Poland's future integration. Nevertheless, barring some unexpected change in the leadership and policies of the PZPR, it seems unlikely that there will be any rapid or radical change in the degree or nature of Poland's integration with the communist system or with the West. It seems most likely that Poland will maintain close economic and political ties with the communist world while slowly increasing its trade with the West, entering into new forms of economic co-operation with Western economic firms and governmental organizations, and, when perceived by the elite as beneficial, engaging in more friendly political and cultural relations with the West. In any case, developments both within the communist system and the Atlantic community will be at least as important as developments within Poland itself in determining Poland's future status.

APPENDIX: SELECTED DATA TABLES

TABLE 1. Proportion of Total Polish Trade with Major
Trading Partners

State	1928		1937	
	Import	Export	Import	Export
	%	%	%	%
United Kingdom	9.3	9.0	11.9	18.3
Germany	26.9	34.3	14.5	14.5
United States	13.9	0.8	11.9	8.4
Belgium	2.0	2.3	4.5	5.8
Netherlands	4.1	3.1	4.6	5.1
Austria	6.6	12.4	4.6	4.9
Sweden	2.1	4.4	3.0	6.3
Czechoslovakia	6.3	11.8	3.5	4.3
France	7.4	1.7	3.2	4.1
Italy	2.5	2.0	2.6	4.5
British India	3.3	0.1	3.6	0.8
Argentina	1.3	0.3	2.8	1.7
Norway	0.5	0.9	1.5	1.8
Australia	0.7	0.0	3.1	0.1
Switzerland	2.6	0.7	1.4	1.8
Denmark	1.6	3.1	1.3	1.3
Egypt	0.4	0.1	1.4	0.8
Brazil	0.7	0.1	1.5	0.7
Finland	0.1	1.0	0.2	1.7
Bulgaria	0.2	0.1	1.2	0.7
Netherlands Indies	0.2	0.3	1.5	0.2
Rumania	1.1	2.2	0.7	0.9
U.S.S.R.	1.2	1.5	1.2	0.4
South Africa	0.1	0.1	0.9	0.6
Palestine	0.0	0.0	0.5	0.8
Greece	0.1	0.1	0.9	0.4
Hungary	1.3	1.7	0.6	0.6
Japan	0.0	0.4	0.3	0.8
Spain	0.1	0.2	0.4	0.6
China	0.1	0.4	0.3	0.6
Yugoslavia	0.3	1.0	0.4	0.5
Turkey	0.1	0.1	0.8	0.1
Belgian Congo	0.0	0.0	0.7	0.2

TABLE 1 (Continued)

State	1928		1937	
	Import	Export	Import	Export
	%	%	%	%
Colombia	0.0	0.0	0.7	0.2
British Malaya	0.0	0.0	0.7	0.1
Chile	1.2	0.0	0.8	0.0
Portugal	0.1	0.0	0.3	0.4
New Zealand	0.0	0.0	0.7	0.0
Canada	0.3	0.0	0.5	0.1
Iran	0.0	0.1	0.1	0.5
Mexico	0.2	0.0	0.3	0.2
Latvia	0.5	2.4	0.1	0.4
Estonia	0.1	0.3	0.2	0.2

Source: Concise Statistical Yearbook of Poland, 1938, p. 157.
Italics indicate states currently members of the communist system.

TABLE 2. Proportion of Polish Imports of Selected
Commodities from Major Suppliers, 1937

Cotton and waste (11.4%)—U.S. (49.1%), Egypt (12.3%),
British India (10.2%), Brazil (8.7%)

Machines and electrical equipment (9.4%)—Germany
(47.8%), United Kingdom (13.7%), U.S. (8.3%), Sweden
(6.4%), Austria (6.3%), Switzerland (3.9%)

Wool and waste (8.5%)—Australia (34.4%), United Kingdom (19.3%), Belgium (12.6%), Argentina (10.0%),
New Zealand (7.9%)

Scrap iron (6.9%)—U.S. (36.9%), Netherlands (21.5%),
United Kingdom (9.5%), Belgium (9.4%), Denmark
(6.9%)

Chemicals and pharmaceuticals (5.4%)—Germany (31.2%),
Argentina (8.9%), United Kingdom (7.9%), Belgium
(7.9%), France (7.9%), Switzerland (7.3%)

Raw hides and skins (3.8%)—Argentina (33.0%), Colombia (15.1%), Netherlands (14.2%), Union of South Africa
(12.2%), Belgium (7.3%)

Transportation equipment (3.4%)—Germany (37.5%), U.S.
(21.6%), United Kingdom (19.5%)

Ores, slag, ashes (2.7%)—U.S.S.R. (19.5%), Sweden (14.8%),
Germany (7.9%), Mexico (6.5%), United Kingdom
(6.5%)

Yarns, tops (2.5%)—United Kingdom (35.3%), Austria
(15.3%), Germany (12.1%), France (9.9%)

Rags (2.3%)—United Kingdom (32.8%), Netherlands
(16.6%), Belgium (14.8%)

Copper and copper sheets (2.3%)—Chile (33.4%), Belgium
(23.3%), U.S. (20.2%), Canada (18.4%)

Paper (2.1%)—Germany (34.9%), Czechoslovakia (22.8%),
Sweden (19.7%)

The percentage figure immediately following each commodity
group shows the share of that group's value of total imports.
The figure following each state is the percentage of that state's
share of Polish imports of the given commodity.

Source: Concise Statistical Yearbook of Poland, 1938, pp. 163–
64. (Unfortunately, data on the relationship of these imports
to total domestic consumption of these commodities are not
readily available.)

TABLE 3. Polish Foreign Trade[a]

Year	Total trade				With communist countries					With noncommunist countries				
	Turnover (million zloty)	Import (million zloty)	Export (million zloty)	Balance	Import (million zloty)	(%)	Export (million zloty)	(%)	Balance	Import (million zloty)	(%)	Export (million zloty)	(%)	Balance
1946	1,089.3	583.1	506.2	−76.9	456.3	78.2	302.9	59.9	−153.4	126.8	21.8	203.3	40.1	+76.5
1947	2,265.6	1,280.6	985.0	−295.6	442.3	34.5	436.2	44.3	−6.1	838.3	65.5	548.8	55.7	−289.5
1948	4,190.7	2,065.6	2,125.1	+59.5	981.7	47.5	939.7	44.2	−42.0	1,083.9	52.5	1,185.4	55.8	+101.5
1949	5,005.1	2,529.8	2,475.3	−54.5	1,077.6	42.6	1,123.0	45.4	+45.4	1,452.2	57.4	1,352.3	54.6	−99.9
1950	5,209.6	2,672.6	2,537.0	−135.6	1,633.2	61.1	1,443.3	56.9	−189.9	1,039.4	38.9	1,093.7	43.1	+54.3
1951	6,743.2	3,696.6	3,046.6	−650.0	2,140.7	57.9	1,737.3	57.0	−403.4	1,555.9	42.1	1,309.3	43.0	−246.6
1952	6,553.6	3,451.9	3,101.7	−350.2	2,330.5	67.5	2,021.1	65.5	−309.4	1,121.4	32.5	1,080.6	34.5	−40.8
1953	6,420.9	3,097.0	3,323.9	+226.9	2,223.6	71.8	2,275.4	68.5	+51.8	873.4	28.2	1,048.5	31.5	+175.1
1954	7,089.0	3,613.8	3,475.2	−138.6	2,565.1	71.0	2,406.9	69.3	−158.2	1,048.7	29.0	1,068.3	30.7	+19.6
1955	7,405.9	3,727.2	3,678.7	−48.5	2,419.8	64.9	2,313.4	62.9	−106.4	1,307.4	35.1	1,365.3	37.1	+57.9
1956	8,026.4	4,087.4	3,939.0	−148.4	2,709.6	66.3	2,320.7	59.0	−388.9	1,377.8	33.7	1,618.3	41.1	+240.5
1957	8,906.0	5,006.1	3,899.9	−1106.2	3,112.2	62.2	2,311.8	59.3	−800.4	1,893.9	37.8	1,588.1	40.7	−305.8
1958	9,144.8	4,907.3	4,237.5	−669.8	2,857.4	58.2	2,481.6	58.6	−375.8	2,049.9	41.8	1,755.9	41.4	−294.0
1959	10,258.9	5,678.4	4,580.5	−1097.9	3,692.0	65.0	2,727.8	60.6	−964.2	1,986.4	35.0	1,852.7	39.4	−133.7
1960	11,282.0	5,979.9	5,302.1	−677.8	3,758.9	62.9	3,304.5	62.3	−454.4	2,221.0	37.1	1,997.6	37.7	−223.4
1961	12,761.1	6,746.8	6,014.3	−732.5	4,119.1	61.1	3,666.2	61.0	−452.9	2,627.7	38.9	2,348.1	39.0	−279.6
1962	14,126.1	7,541.6	6,584.5	−957.1	4,984.7	66.1	4,137.2	62.8	−847.5	2,556.9	33.9	2,447.3	37.2	−109.6
1963	14,996.2	7,916.1	7,080.1	−836.0	5,304.4	67.0	4,492.3	63.4	−811.7	2,612.1	33.0	2,587.8	36.6	−24.3
1964	16,674.7	8,289.0	8,385.7	+96.7	5,224.6	63.0	5,402.5	64.4	+177.9	3,064.4	37.0	2,983.2	35.6	−81.2
1965	18,272.6	9,361.2	8,911.4	−449.8	6,190.0	66.1	5,634.7	63.0	−555.3	3,171.2	33.9	3,276.7	36.8	+105.5
1966	19,064.6	9,976.2	9,088.4	−887.8	6,415.4	64.3	5,600.6	61.6	−814.8	3,560.8	35.7	3,487.8	38.4	−73.0

[a]Trade is given in terms of current prices for foreign exchange zloty (4 = $1.00 U.S.).
Sources: Glowny Urzad Statystycny, Rocznik Statystyczny, 1959, pp. 250–53; Maly Rocznik Statystyczny, 1967, pp. 175–77; Rocznik Statystyczny Handlu Zagranicznego, 1965, pp. 10, 12–13. Import and export percentages calculated from data.

TABLE 4. Polish Trade with the Communist-Ruled States, 1949–66[a]

Year	U.S.S.R.				Albania				Bulgaria			
	Import		Export		Import		Export		Import		Export	
	(million zloty)	(%)	(million zloty)	(%)	(million zloty)	(%)	(million zloty)	(%)	(million zloty)	(%)	(million zloty)	(%)
1937	—	1.2	—	0.4	—	—	—	—	—	1.2	—	0.7
1949	474.4	18.8	481.3	19.4	1.8	0.1	5.0	0.2	34.2	1.4	54.7	2.2
1950	769.5	28.8	616.3	24.3	2.0	0.1	11.2	0.4	48.1	1.8	46.3	1.8
1953	1,053.6	34.0	1,098.1	33.0	3.2	0.1	11.1	0.3	38.3	1.2	58.4	1.8
1955	1,254.3	33.7	1,122.0	30.5	4.9	0.1	10.6	0.3	27.8	0.7	38.3	1.0
1956	1,377.1	33.7	1,081.0	27.4	4.6	0.1	7.6	0.2	42.3	1.0	25.7	0.7
1957	1,687.5	33.7	1,033.9	26.5	8.2	0.2	12.6	0.3	58.5	1.2	47.8	1.2
1958	1,335.9	27.2	1,060.8	25.0	7.6	0.2	17.6	0.4	74.9	1.5	68.5	1.6
1959	1,809.2	31.9	1,251.9	27.3	9.2	0.2	16.8	0.4	88.5	1.6	68.0	1.5
1960	1,861.1	31.1	1,560.9	29.4	12.2	0.2	13.2	0.2	10.7	1.3	110.5	2.1
1961	1,959.0	29.0	1,940.0	32.3	15.9	0.2	14.9	0.2	83.2	1.2	86.4	1.4
1962	2,311.4	30.6	2,274.6	34.5	20.5	0.3	14.8	0.2	124.8	1.7	97.1	1.5
1963	2,588.7	32.7	2,469.8	34.9	14.6	0.2	21.2	0.3	131.5	1.7	138.0	1.9
1964	2,569.7	31.0	2,887.1	34.4	24.1	0.3	27.4	0.3	127.5	1.5	141.0	1.7
1965	2,913.7	31.1	3,125.5	35.1	25.1	0.3	20.5	0.2	159.1	1.7	179.7	2.0
1966	3,166.8	31.7	2,964.7	32.6	17.5	0.2	19.8	0.2	175.2	1.8	178.2	2.0

TABLE 4 (Continued)

Year	Czechoslovakia Import (million zloty)	(%)	Export (million zloty)	(%)	German Democratic Rep. Import (million zloty)	(%)	Export (million zloty)	(%)	Hungary Import (million zloty)	(%)	Export (million zloty)	(%)
1937	—	3.5	—	4.3	—	7.5	—	10.5	—	0.6	—	0.6
1949	278.2	11.0	213.0	8.6	189.3	7.5	259.0	10.5	46.6	1.8	54.0	2.2
1950	351.6	13.2	232.7	9.2	307.7	11.5	352.3	13.9	99.0	3.7	107.7	4.2
1953	328.5	10.6	380.9	11.5	512.3	16.5	444.9	13.4	125.4	4.0	109.7	3.3
1955	318.7	8.2	301.2	8.2	487.3	13.1	500.3	13.6	122.4	3.3	105.6	2.9
1956	411.5	10.1	304.9	7.7	541.0	13.2	430.0	10.9	92.3	2.3	99.1	2.5
1957	308.5	6.2	244.4	6.3	659.5	13.2	501.3	12.9	83.0	1.7	130.4	3.3
1958	377.8	7.7	290.0	6.8	621.9	12.7	425.5	10.0	135.4	2.8	114.6	2.7
1959	451.6	8.0	322.5	7.0	749.0	13.2	547.5	11.9	146.3	2.6	148.3	3.2
1960	508.5	8.5	452.2	8.5	745.6	12.5	498.6	9.4	184.3	3.1	186.0	3.5
1961	651.4	9.7	587.2	9.8	811.0	12.0	438.8	7.3	235.9	3.5	220.4	3.7
1962	794.6	10.5	583.4	8.9	939.6	12.5	470.4	7.1	272.7	3.6	254.5	3.9
1963	771.9	9.7	579.0	8.2	1,013.5	12.8	481.9	6.8	303.5	3.8	316.1	4.5
1964	772.5	9.3	783.4	9.3	943.3	11.4	658.0	7.8	330.5	4.0	359.3	4.3
1965	976.4	10.4	833.8	9.4	1,085.4	11.6	612.6	6.9	422.8	4.5	343.7	3.9
1966	932.5	9.3	713.2	7.8	1,121.2	11.2	642.4	7.1	416.3	4.2	366.1	4.0

145

TABLE 4 (Continued)

Year	Rumania				Yugoslavia				Mongolia			
	Import		Export		Import		Export		Import		Export	
	(million zloty)	(%)	(million zloty)	(%)	(million zloty)	(%)	(million zloty)	(%)	(million zloty)	(%)	(million zloty)	(%)
1937	—	0.7	—	0.9	—	0.4	—	0.5	—	—	—	—
1949	36.0	1.4	37.4	1.5	—	—	—	—	—	—	—	—
1950	46.6	1.7	52.0	2.0	—	—	—	—	—	—	—	—
1953	53.0	1.7	37.8	1.1	—	—	—	—	—	—	—	—
1955	47.6	1.3	50.2	1.4	15.2	0.4	14.8	0.4	—	—	—	—
1956	56.6	1.4	76.5	1.9	35.7	0.9	28.6	0.7	—	—	—	—
1957	62.2	1.2	68.2	1.7	71.2	1.4	72.8	1.9	—	—	—	—
1958	49.2	1.0	54.4	1.3	89.2	1.8	136.2	3.2	—	—	—	—
1959	84.4	1.5	70.6	1.5	100.1	1.8	82.6	1.8	5.0	0.1	4.4	0.1
1960	82.1	1.4	92.8	1.8	61.2	1.0	147.0	2.8	7.8	0.1	12.3	0.2
1961	96.2	1.4	130.1	2.3	156.2	2.3	104.9	1.7	8.9	0.1	12.3	0.2
1962	160.8	2.1	140.4	2.1	156.6	2.1	126.2	1.9	8.4	0.1	10.2	0.2
1963	133.1	1.7	164.7	2.3	139.3	1.8	132.8	1.9	11.5	0.1	20.2	0.3
1964	118.0	1.4	158.6	1.9	161.8	1.9	222.7	2.7	9.4	0.1	20.5	0.2
1965	178.7	1.9	143.2	1.6	252.2	2.7	216.4	2.4	13.8	0.1	20.8	0.2
1966	164.1	1.6	184.9	2.0	226.5	2.3	300.0	3.3	9.9	0.1	11.1	0.1

TABLE 4 (Continued)

Year	Chinese People's Rep.				Korean Dem. P. Rep.				Viet. Dem. Rep.				Cuba			
	Import		Export		Import		Export		Import		Export		Import		Export	
	(million złoty)	(%)	(million złoty)	(%)	(million złoty)	(%)	(million złoty)	(%)	(million złoty)	(%)	(million złoty)	(%)	(million złoty)	(%)	(million złoty)	(%)
1937	—	0.3	—	—	—	—	—	—	—	—	—	—	—	—	—	—
1949	—	—	—	0.6	—	—	—	—	—	—	—	—	—	—	—	—
1950	8.6	0.3	24.8	1.0	—	—	—	—	—	—	—	—	—	—	0.3	0.0
1953	109.3	3.5	126.4	3.8	0.9	0.0	8.2	0.2	—	—	—	—	—	—	—	—
1955	140.7	3.8	139.5	3.8	4.5	0.1	31.0	0.8	—	—	—	—	—	—	—	—
1956	140.9	3.4	201.2	5.1	10.6	0.2	52.5	1.3	—	—	—	—	—	—	—	—
1957	149.3	3.0	179.4	4.6	3.3	0.1	5.6	0.1	13.3	0.3	14.0	0.4	—	—	—	—
1958	145.0	3.0	288.6	6.8	9.8	0.2	7.1	0.2	14.1	0.3	13.8	0.3	—	—	—	—
1959	224.2	3.9	171.5	3.7	7.5	0.1	26.0	0.6	14.8	0.3	17.7	0.3	—	—	0.0	0.0
1960	185.5	3.1	199.8	3.8	11.4	0.2	5.4	0.1	24.4	0.4	25.9	0.5	39.0	0.7	16.3	0.3
1961	82.7	1.2	106.8	1.8	15.9	0.2	5.7	0.1	6.4	0.1	17.3	0.3	97.5	1.4	90.2	1.5
1962	91.0	1.2	60.2	0.9	15.4	0.2	13.1	0.2	11.6	0.2	7.5	0.1	76.4	1.0	81.2	1.2
1963	99.0	1.3	44.8	0.6	15.0	0.2	17.6	0.2	11.7	0.1	5.3	0.1	69.4	0.9	97.0	1.4
1964	99.9	1.2	59.9	0.7	24.6	0.2	16.4	0.2	20.9	0.3	8.5	0.1	31.4	0.4	55.3	0.7
1965	99.9	1.1	76.9	0.9	25.6	0.3	19.3	0.2	20.5	0.2	16.1	0.2	17.1	0.2	21.0	0.2
1966	90.9	0.9	118.3	1.3	—	0.3	23.1	0.3	14.9	0.1	42.1	0.5	53.5	0.5	31.3	0.3

[a] Exports and imports given in figures of current foreign exchange zloty (4 = $1.00 U.S.)

Sources: Concise Statistical Yearbook of Poland, 1938, p. 157; Glowny Urzad Statystyczny, Rocznik Statystyczny, 1959, pp. 250-53; Rocznik Statystyczny, 1966, pp. 237-38; Mały Rocznik Statystyczny, 1967, pp. 175-77. (Percentages calculated from data.)

TABLE 5. Proportion of Polish Trade with Most Important Trading Partners

Country	1949		1953		1955		1957		1962		1966	
	Imp.	Exp.	Imp.	Exp.	Imp.	Exp.	Imp.	Exp.	Imp.	Exp.	Imp.	Exp.
	(%)	(%)	(%)	(%)	(%)	(%)	(%)	(%)	(%)	(%)	(%)	(%)
U.S.S.R.	18.8	24.3	34.0	33.0	33.7	30.5	33.7	26.5	30.6	34.5	31.7	32.6
G.D.R.	7.5	10.5	16.5	13.4	13.1	13.6	13.2	12.9	12.5	7.1	11.2	7.1
Czechoslovakia	11.0	8.6	10.6	11.5	8.2	8.2	6.2	6.3	10.5	8.9	9.3	7.8
Great Britain	13.4	10.1	7.5	7.3	7.5	8.5	6.5	6.5	6.3	6.3	6.4	6.4
Hungary	1.8	2.2	4.0	3.3	3.3	2.9	1.7	3.3	3.6	3.9	4.2	4.0
G.D.R.	1.8	3.0	1.9	2.0	2.5	3.2	4.4	5.1	3.3	5.1	2.7	5.4
Yugoslavia	–	–	–	–	0.1	0.4	1.4	1.9	2.1	1.9	2.3	3.3
U.S.	2.3	0.7	0.1	1.6	2.7	2.5	4.5	2.7	4.2	2.6	1.8	3.5
Italy	2.9	4.3	1.5	1.7	0.9	0.7	1.3	1.0	1.6	2.4	2.8	2.5
France	7.1	6.1	1.6	1.6	3.7	1.4	1.8	4.1	1.4	1.5	2.4	1.6
Austria	1.7	3.0	2.7	2.9	2.0	3.2	2.8	3.3	1.6	2.0	2.3	1.7
Bulgaria	1.4	2.2	1.2	1.8	0.7	1.0	1.2	1.2	1.7	1.9	1.8	2.0
Rumania	1.4	1.5	1.7	1.1	1.3	1.4	1.2	1.7	2.1	2.1	1.6	2.0
Sweden	5.3	7.0	3.5	2.6	1.6	2.3	1.7	1.7	1.1	2.0	1.2	1.6
Denmark	2.7	4.6	0.7	1.3	0.5	1.2	0.4	1.2	1.1	1.4	1.1	1.2
Holland	4.8	4.1	0.7	0.6	1.8	0.8	2.1	0.5	0.5	0.7	1.1	1.1
India	–	–	0.0	0.1	0.1	0.1	2.4	0.8	1.0	1.2	0.8	1.5

TABLE 5 (Continued)

China (Peo. Rep.)	—	—	0.0	0.1	0.1	0.1	2.4	0.8	1.0	1.2	0.8	1.5
Switzerland	2.3	1.2	1.5	0.8	1.4	0.8	0.9	1.0	1.2	1.2	1.2	0.9
Canada	—	—	0.0	0.0	0.3	0.1	1.5	0.1	1.6	0.3	1.3	0.6
Finland	1.6	3.2	1.6	3.7	1.7	3.6	2.0	4.3	1.2	1.4	0.8	1.0
U.A.R. (Egypt)	0.7	0.3	0.4	0.5	1.0	0.4	1.4	0.7	0.4	0.8	0.6	0.8
Belgium	1.8	1.2	1.0	0.5	1.3	0.4	1.1	0.5	0.3	0.6	0.6	0.6
Greece	—	—	0.2	0.2	0.0	0.0	0.0	0.1	0.3	0.5	0.5	0.5
Spain	—	—	—	—	—	—	0.1	0.1	0.4	0.5	0.6	0.4
Argentina	1.7	0.0	1.2	0.5	3.1	2.4	0.4	0.3	1.0	0.1	0.9	0.1
Australia	—	—	0.0	0.0	0.0	0.0	0.0	0.1	0.9	0.1	0.8	0.1
Norway	2.2	2.4	0.6	0.8	0.5	0.4	0.3	0.3	0.3	0.4	0.4	0.5
Cuba	—	—	—	—	—	—	—	—	1.0	1.2	0.5	0.3
Pakistan	0.4	—	0.4	0.2	0.5	0.3	0.3	0.1	0.3	0.1	0.4	0.4

Countries in italics are members of the communist system.

Sources: Glowny Urzad Statystyczny, *Rocznik Statystyczny, 1959,* pp. 252–54; *Rocznik Statystyczny, 1964,* pp. 325–26; *Mały Rocznik Statystyczny, 1967,* pp. 175–78.

Table 6. Proportion of Polish Imports from Major
Suppliers for Selected Commodities

Proportion of Imports for 1955

Crude oil—U.S.S.R. (75.6%), Hungary (9.7%), Rumania (6.6%), Australia (1.9%)

Petroleum products—Rumania (31.7%), U.S.S.R. (27.0%), G.D.R. (25.9%), Hungary (5.6%)

Iron ore—U.S.S.R. (69.3%), Sweden (10.3%), China (5.5%), W. Germany (2.4%)

Zinc concentrate—U.S.S.R. (44.7%), Bulgaria (15.0%), Italy (13.7%)

Cotton—U.S.S.R. (17.9%), Egypt (7.4%), China (3.2%), Turkey (2.6%)

Wool—Great Britain (88.6%), Argentina (7.8%)

Artificial fertilizer—G.D.R. (59.6%), France (20.0%), U.S.S.R. (11.0%)

Cellulose—Finland (88.1%), Austria (4.4%)

Rubber—Great Britain (44.6%), U.S.S.R. (17.6%), Holland (12.2%), G.D.R. (11.9%),

Fats—Norway (33.4%), U.S.S.R. (26.8%)

Tobacco—Turkey (44.2%), Bulgaria (16.2%)

Coffee—Brazil (92.0%), Belgium (8.0%)

Wheat—France (35.6%), Argentina (31.6%), U.S.S.R. (12.0%)

Proportion of Imports for 1958

Crude oil—U.S.S.R. (94.5%), Bulgaria (3.7%)

Petroleum products—U.S.S.R. (76.0%), Rumania (15.2%), Hungary (2.7%)

Iron ore—U.S.S.R. (74.3%), Sweden (10.6%), Brazil (6.3%)

Milled products—G.D.R. (31.0%), U.S.S.R. (17.3%), Czechoslovakia (16.8%), Austria (10.8%), Belgium (7.3%)

Manganese ore—U.S.S.R. (94.7%), Brazil (3.2%)

Zinc concentrate—Bulgaria (67.3%), U.S.S.R. (16.8%), Korea (9.3%)

Copper—U.S.S.R. (23.0%), Great Britain (21.7%), W. Germany (18.7%), Finland (11.7%), Switzerland (8.8%)

TABLE 6 (Continued)

Natural rubber—Great Britain (66.2%), China (22.8%), Malaysia (6.9%)

Synthetic rubber—G.D.R. (57.9%), U.S.S.R. (34.2%), U.S. (4.7%)

Cellulose—Finland (87.2%), Yugoslavia (7.7%)

Cotton—U.S.S.R. (47.6%), U.S. (37.2%), Egypt (9.9%), China (1.4%)

Wool—Great Britain (77.8%), Argentina (11.9%)

Fats—U.S. (52.7%), China (10.7%), Hungary (8.6%), Argentina (7.8%), Great Britain (5.5%)

Tobacco—Bulgaria (35.1%), Turkey (27.6%), China (17.0%), Yugoslavia (16.9%)

Coffee—Brazil (100.0%)

Wheat—U.S. (64.5%), U.S.S.R. (35.5%)

Proportion of Imports for 1963

Crude oil—U.S.S.R. (100.0%)

Petroleum products—U.S.S.R. (79.6%), Rumania (9.7%), G.D.R. (3.3%), Hungary (2.5%)

Iron ore—U.S.S.R. (80.5%), Sweden (6.1%), Brazil (4.1%)

Manganese ore—U.S.S.R. (80.9%), Cuba (8.9%), India (7.3%)

Milled products—Czechoslovakia (55.5%), U.S.S.R. (10.6%), Austria (5.9%), Hungary (5.8%), W. Germany (5.6%), Great Britain (4.5%), G.D.R. (4.1%)

Copper—Great Britain (27.5%), U.S.S.R. (22.5%), Holland (12.0%), Spain (11.1%), W. Germany (9.2%), Finland (8.6%)

Artificial fertilizer—G.D.R. (51.5%), U.S.S.R. (18.5%) Morocco (16.5%), China (7.1%)

Natural rubber—Great Britain (43.4%), Malaysia (22.7%), Ceylon (18.2%), Indonesia (11.7%)

Synthetic rubber—G.D.R. (47.6%), W. Germany (15.2%), Great Britain (13.5%)

Cellulose—Finland (61.4%), Norway (16.0%), Sweden (15.2%)

Cotton—U.S.S.R. (45.2%), U.S. (17.6%), U.A.R. (9.0%)

Wool—Australia (42.6%), Argentina (19.9%), New Zealand (9.1%), Great Britain (5.6%)

Table 6 (Continued)

Fats—U.S. (45.0%), Argentina (16.4%), Norway (6.8%)
Wheat—U.S. (36.8%), France (30.9%), Canada (11.9%),
U.S.S.R. (9.2%)
Coffee—Brazil (65.7%), Colombia (19.3%), India (5.9%)

Proportion of Imports for 1966

Crude oil—U.S.S.R. (100.0%)
Petroleum products—U.S.S.R. (64.4%), Rumania (12.3%)
Iron ore—U.S.S.R. (79.2%), Sweden (8.5%), India (3.6%),
Guinea (3.5%)
Manganese ore—U.S.S.R. (71.3%), Cuba (13.2%), India
(10.6%)
Zinc concentrate—Canada (39.7%), Holland (15.7%),
U.S. (13.7%), Yugoslavia (8.2%)
Milled products—Czechoslovakia (50.0%), U.S.S.R.
(14.3%), Hungary (7.1%), Austria (6.1%), W. Germany (6.0%)
Copper—U.S.S.R. (45.9%), Great Britain (23.8%), W.
Germany (11.7%)
Artificial fertilizer—G.D.R. (34.1%), U.S.S.R. (19.6%),
Morocco (15.5%)
Natural rubber—Great Britain (48.5%), Indonesia
. (18.6%), Ceylon (16.3%)
Synthetic rubber—G.D.R. (51.1%), Great Britain
(17.0%), U.S.S.R. (12.6%)
Cellulose—Finland (54.6%), Norway (19.3%), Austria
(13.8%)
Cotton—U.S.S.R. (55.9%), U.A.R. (0.1%), U.S. (6.3%),
Iran (5.6%)
Wool—Australia (41.6%), Argentina (17.3%), Great
Britain (16.3%)
Tobacco—Greece (30.0%), Bulgaria (29.1%), Yugoslavia
(23.0%)
Wheat—Mexico (34.8%), Canada (22.1%), France
(20.3%), U.S. (0.6%)

Sources: Glowny Urzad Statystyczny. *Rocznik Statystyczny, 1956*, pp. 250–51; *Rocznik Statystyczny, 1959*, pp. 255–57; *Rocznik Statystyczny, 1964*, pp. 331–34; *Rocznik Statystyczny, 1966*, pp. 366–69.

TABLE 7. Proportion of Polish Exports to Major Buyers
for Selected Commodities

Proportion of Exports for 1955

Coal—U.S.S.R. (34.0%), G.D.R. (15.7%), Czechoslovakia
(15.3%)
Coke—G.D.R. (47.3%), U.S.S.R. (19.4%), Hungary
(14.9%), Rumania (10.5%)
Milled products—U.S.S.R. (23.3%), China (24.0%),
Bulgaria (9.7%), G.D.R. (6.1%)
Tin and tin sheets—U.S.S.R. (53.0%), Czechoslovakia
(19.1%), Hungary (7.4%), China (6.5%)
Sugar—U.S.S.R. (57.0%), China (11.3%)
Textiles (cotton)—Turkey (15.5%), G.D.R. (13.6%),
China (9.0%), U.S.S.R. (8.8%), Indonesia (5.8%)
Textiles (wool)—U.S.S.R. (72.1%), G.D.R. (9.0%)
Soda—U.S.S.R. (71.8%), Czechoslovakia (8.1%), Hungary
(7.9%)
Locomotives—U.S.S.R. (100.0%)
Freight cars—U.S.S.R. (76.5%), Bulgaria (23.5%)
Ships—U.S.S.R. (84.4%), China (15.1%)
Meat—Great Britain (58.6%), U.S. (17.1%), U.S.S.R.
(8.3%), G.D.R. (5.7%)
Machine tools—Argentina (44.0%), U.S.S.R. (13.7%),
China (10.5%), Brazil (7.1%), Turkey (6.6%)

Proportion of Exports for 1958

Coal—U.S.S.R. (22.0%), G.D.R. (11.1%), Czechoslovakia
(9.6%), Finland (8.7%), W. Germany (7.9%), Den-
mark (7.4%), Austria (6.2%), Argentina (5.3%),
France (4.5%), Hungary (4.0%), Sweden (3.9%)
Lignite—G.D.R. (100.0%)
Coke—G.D.R. (38.0%), U.S.S.R. (32.8%), Hungary
(13.3%), Rumania (4.4%)
Milled products—China (16.6%), U.S.S.R. (16.3%),
Brazil (11.6%), Czechoslovakia (10.6%), Bulgaria
(7.2%), Yugoslavia (7.2%), Rumania (5.5%), W. Ger-
many (5.1%), G.D.R. (2.6%)
Zinc and plate—U.S.S.R. (33.3%), Czechoslovakia
(15.6%), Great Britain (12.2%), W. Germany (7.8%),
Hungary (6.6%)

TABLE 7 (Continued)

Locomotives—India (51.9%), China (48.1%)

Railroad freight cars—U.S.S.R. (62.9%), Yugoslavia (25.6%), G.D.R. (6.2%)

Railroad passenger cars—U.S.S.R. (100.0%)

Ships—U.S.S.R. (61.0%), China (15.9%), Egypt (12.8%), Brazil (7.8%)

Machine tools—China (30.7%), U.S.S.R. (21.1%), Czechoslovakia (13.8%), Yugoslavia (3.3%), Turkey (2.6%), G.D.R. (2.5%)

Soda—U.S.S.R. (40.7%), Czechoslovakia (15.1%), Brazil (14.8%), W. Germany (12.3%)

Cotton textiles—Morocco (20.0%), Yugoslavia (12.6%), Haiti (9.5%), Irak (6.4%), Vietnam (6.2%), Sweden (5.9%)

Wool textiles—U.S.S.R. (66.1%), Mongolia (2.9%), Albania (2.5%)

Sugar—U.S.S.R. (22.5%), Great Britain (10.8%), Yugoslavia (10.4%), China (8.6%)

Bacon—Great Britain (100.0%)

Canned meat—W. Germany (47.0%), Great Britain (29.6%), U.S. (23.0%)

Canned hams—U.S. (75.3%), Great Britain (23.0%)

Fowl—W. Germany (31.0%), Czechoslovakia (5.6%), G.D.R. (4.8%)

Proportion of Exports for 1963

Coal—U.S.S.R. (28.7%), Denmark (13.3%), G.D.R. (9.0%), Finland (8.6%), Austria (8.5%), Czechoslovakia (7.6%), Hungary (4.9%), Italy (4.3%)

Coke—G.D.R. (31.3%), Sweden (26.4%), Austria (18.6%)

Sulphur—Czechoslovakia (44.4%), Sweden (14.6%), Austria (14.2%), W. Germany (13.2%)

Milled products—Czechoslovakia (20.5%), U.S.S.R. (13.0%), Yugoslavia (8.1%), Great Britain (7.2%)

Zinc and plate—U.S.S.R. (35.3%), Czechoslovakia (18.6%), Hungary (9.2%)

Soda—U.S.S.R. (21.1%), Czechoslovakia (17.9%), W. Germany (12.0%), Finland (9.4%)

TABLE 7 (Continued)

Machine tools—Czechoslovakia (24.7%), U.S.S.R. (13.3%), India (13.0%), Italy (5.4%), Yugoslavia (4.6%), Hungary (4.1%), U.A.R. (4.1%), Great Britain (3.7%)

Railroad freight cars—U.S.S.R. (70.1%), Hungary (23.9%)

Railroad passenger cars—U.S.S.R. (94.7%), Greece (5.3%)

Trucks—Bulgaria (46.0%), Hungary (24.8%), Cuba (10.6%), Czechoslovakia (10.3%), Turkey (5.5%)

Cars—Hungary (43.2%), Bulgaria (21.9%), Rumania (12.4%), China (8.4%)

Ships—U.S.S.R. (78.9%), Cuba (10.6%), China (5.3%), Indonesia (5.2%)

Frozen meat—Italy (23.4%), Spain (18.8%), Czechoslovakia (17.8%)

Canned meat—Great Britain (37.2%), W. Germany (29.3%), U.S. (24.9%)

Canned ham—U.S. (70.3%), Great Britain (16.4%)

Proportion of Exports for 1965

Coal—U.S.S.R. (31.0%), Denmark (11.9%), G.D.R. (9.5%), Finland (8.6%), Czechoslovakia (7.6%), Austria (7.1%)

Coke—G.D.R. (36.9%), U.S.S.R. (28.4%) Hungary (11.2%)

Sulphur—Czechoslovakia (55.0%), W. Germany (15.0%), Austria (11.7%), Sweden (8.7%)

Machine tools (pieces)—Czechoslovakia (11.5%), India (9.0%), U.A.R. (8.1%), G.D.R. (6.5%)

Railroad freight cars—U.S.S.R. (75.0%), Hungary (22.2%)

Railroad passenger cars—U.S.S.R. (100.0%)

Trucks—Bulgaria (50.0%), Czechoslovakia (26.3%), Hungary (13.7%), U.A.R. (6.5%)

Milled products—Czechoslovakia (19.1%), U.S.S.R. (16.1%), U.S. (8.4%)

Zinc and plate—U.S.S.R. (55.9%), Czechoslovakia

Table 7 (Continued)

(17.6%), Hungary (8.0%)

Soda—U.S.S.R. (39.3%), Czechoslovakia (19.2%), W. Germany (13.7%), Sweden (6.8%)

Sugar—Great Britain (12.1%), Ceylon (10.6%), Sudan (10.4%)

Cotton textiles—Indonesia (15.7%), Irak (9.3%), Canada (6.7%)

Wool textiles—U.S.S.R. (51.8%), China (24.0%)

Sources: Glowny Urzad Statystyczny, *Rocznik Statystyczny, 1956,* pp. 253–56; *Rocznik Statystyczny, 1959,* pp. 257–59; *Rocznik Statystyczny, 1964,* pp. 235–41; *Rocznik Statystyczny, 1966,* pp. 370–75.

TABLE 8. Population Growth

Year	Total	Men	Women	Urban No.	Urban %	Rural	Live births Total	Live births Urban	Live births Rural	Deaths Total	Deaths Urban	Deaths Rural	Pop. growth rate Total	Pop. growth rate Urban	Pop. growth rate Rural	Infant mortality Total	Infant mortality Urban	Infant mortality Rural
	(thousands)						*(per thousand population)*											
1921[a]	27,177	13,183	14,044	6,608	24.6	20,250	—	—	—	—	—	—	—	—	—	—	—	—
1931[a]	32,107	15,619	16,488	8,731	27.4	23,185	—	—	—	—	—	—	—	—	—	—	—	—
1946[b]	23,930	10,954	12,976	7,517	31.8	16,109	—	—	—	—	—	—	—	—	—	—	—	—
1950[b]	25,008	11,928	13,080	9,605	39.0	15,009	—	—	—	—	—	—	—	—	—	—	—	—
1960[b]	29,776	14,404	15,372	14,206	48.3	15,200	—	—	—	—	—	—	—	—	—	—	—	—
1931–32[c]	—	—	—	—	—	—	29.8	21.0	33.0	15.3	12.6	16.3	14.5	8.4	16.7	143.0[d]	121.5[d]	148.2
1936–38[c]	—	—	—	—	—	—	25.3	—	—	14.1	—	—	11.2	—	—	139.2[d]	—	—
1938[a]	34,849	17,000	17,849	10,455	30.0	24,394	—	—	—	—	—	—	—	—	—	—	—	—
1949	24,613	11,718	12,895	8,920	36.2	15,693	—	—	—	—	—	—	—	—	—	—	—	—
1950	25,035	11,942	13,093	9,243	36.9	15,792	30.7	30.0	31.2	11.6	10.9	12.1	19.1	19.1	19.1	111.2	102.6	116.0
1951	25,507	12,183	13,324	10,126	39.7	15,381	31.0	30.7	31.2	12.4	11.5	12.9	18.6	19.2	18.3	117.6	106.3	124.6
1952	25,999	12,437	13,562	10,525	40.5	15,474	30.2	29.7	30.6	11.1	10.4	11.6	19.1	19.3	19.0	96.4	88.2	101.7
1953	26,511	12,700	13,811	10,858	41.0	15,653	29.7	29.2	30.0	10.2	9.4	10.7	19.5	19.8	19.3	88.4	80.1	94.0
1954	27,012	12,955	14,057	11,316	41.9	15,696	29.1	28.7	29.3	10.3	9.5	10.9	18.8	19.2	18.4	83.3	75.5	88.7
1955	27,550	13,232	14,318	12,067	43.8	15,483	29.1	28.6	29.5	9.6	8.9	10.1	19.5	19.7	19.4	82.2	73.3	88.3
1956	28,080	13,506	14,574	12,594	44.9	15,486	28.1	26.8	29.1	9.0	8.3	9.5	19.1	18.5	19.6	70.9	64.8	75.4
1957	28,540	13,745	14,795	12,978	45.5	15,562	27.6	26.0	29.0	9.5	8.6	10.3	18.1	17.4	18.7	77.2	70.0	82.6
1958	29,000	13,980	15,020	13,471	46.4	15,529	26.3	24.5	27.8	8.4	7.7	9.0	17.9	16.8	18.8	72.1	64.2	78.2
1959	29,480	14,226	15,254	13,958	47.3	15,522	24.7	22.4	26.8	8.6	7.9	9.3	16.1	14.5	17.5	71.4	64.4	76.6
1960	29,795	14,414	15,381	14,401	48.3	15,394	22.6	19.9	24.9	7.6	7.0	8.0	15.0	12.9	16.9	54.8	49.7	58.5
1961	30,183	14,584	15,549	14,627	48.5	15,506	20.9	18.1	23.6	7.6	6.9	8.2	13.3	11.2	15.4	53.2	47.0	57.7
1962	30,484	14,768	15,716	14,880	48.8	15,604	19.8	16.9	22.4	7.9	7.1	8.6	11.9	9.8	13.8	54.2	47.8	58.8
1963	30,940	15,002	15,938	15,209	49.2	15,731	19.2	16.3	21.9	7.5	6.9	8.0	11.7	9.4	13.9	48.5	44.2	51.6
1964	31,339	15,206	16,133	15,485	49.4	15,854	18.1	15.5	20.5	7.6	7.0	8.1	10.5	8.5	12.4	47.2	41.6	51.3
1965	31,551	15,319	16,232	15,681	49.7	15,870	17.4	14.9	19.7	7.4	6.9	7.8	10.0	8.0	11.9	41.5	38.8	43.4
1966	31,811	15,453	16,358	15,909	50.5	15,902	16.7	14.4	19.1	7.3	7.0	7.8	9.4	7.4	11.3	38.6	35.1	41.2

[a] 1938 borders. [b] Present borders. [c] Annual average. [d] Incomplete data.
Sources: Glowny Urzad Statystyczny, Rocznik Statystyczny, 1966, pp. 13, 46; Maly Rocznik Statystyczny, 1967, pp. 9–10, 22.

TABLE 9. Travel to and from Poland[a]

Year	To Poland		From Poland	
	Total	Czech. convention	Total	Czech. convention
	(thousands)	*(thousands)*	*(thousands)*	*(thousands)*
1956	78.1	42.0	256.7	88.2
1957	115.5	28.5	236.3	21.6
1958	123.1	24.1	163.8	27.7
1959	147.0	25.2	193.7	27.3
1960	184.0	18.8	216.4	45.6
1961	254.8	108.9	371.9	161.5
1962	404.4	221.5	446.5	187.3
1963	285.2	88.1	385.8	100.1
1964	818.3	230.3	568.7	221.7
1965	1086.2	203.4	778.4	253.3
1966	1209.7	170.7	949.0	214.7

[a]The figures above include official travel to and from Poland, foreign students studying in Poland or going abroad to study, and tourist travel. The data include tourists traveling to and from Czechoslovakia under the provisions of a special convention easing travel between the two countries, but do not include similar travel under the provisions of a convention with the German Democratic Republic until 1965. Transit tourist travel is included in the travel to Poland beginning with 1964.

Sources: Glowny Urzad Statystyczny, *Rocznik Statystyczny, 1966,* p. 488; *Maly Rocznik Statystyczny, 1967,* p. 217.

Table 10 (Part I). Rate of Polish Industrial Growth

Year	Per cent
1956	9[a]
1957	10
1958	10
1959	9
1960	11
1961	8
1962	5
1963	9
1964	9
1965	7
1966	10

[a]The figures are rounded off to the nearest percentage in the source cited.

Source: Glowny Urzad Statystyczny, *Maly Rocznik Statystyczny, 1967,* pp. 62-63.

Table 10 (Part II). Indices of Relative Industrial Growth[a]

1950	1955	1956	1957	1958	1959	1960	1961	1962	1963	1964
100	212	231	253	278	304	338	372	404	426	465
47	**100**	109	120	132	144	160	176	191	201	220
43	92	**100**	110	121	132	147	162	175	185	202
39	83	91	**100**	110	120	133	147	160	168	184
36	76	83	91	**100**	109	121	134	145	153	167
33	70	76	84	92	**100**	111	123	133	140	153
30	63	68	75	82	90	**100**	110	120	126	138
27	57	62	68	75	82	91	**100**	108	114	125
25	52	57	63	69	75	84	92	**100**	105	115
23	50	54	59	65	71	79	87	95	**100**	109
22	45	49	54	60	65	73	80	87	92	**100**

[a]Compiled on the base of 100 for each year. (The table should be read horizontally—left or right—from the 100 base figure under each year to compare industrial production in that year with any other year.)

Source: Maly Rocznik Statystyczny, 1965, p. 56.

TABLE 11. Volume of Letters, Periodicals, Packages, Telegrams, and Telephone Calls to and from Poland, 1949 and 1955–66

	Letters[a] (in thousands)		Newspapers & Magazines (in thousands)		Packages (in thousands)		Telegrams (in thousands)		Telephone Calls (in thousands)	
	To Poland	From Poland	To Poland	From Poland	To Poland	From Poland	To Poland	From Poland	To Poland	From Poland
1949	29,767	24,419	16,443	3,069	1,126	18	312	331	57	63
1955	15,584	21,006	55,453	5,492	843	40	483	657	97	206
1956	20,475	23,789	44,514	7,628	874	57	683	926	159	356
1957	27,667	37,972	31,524	11,483	1,499	87	702	754	210	273
1958	25,543	25,012	20,698	18,186	1,553	153	565	619	188	254
1959	29,757	29,920	21,454	20,681	1,680	226	510	579	201	259
1960	28,064	35,879	22,976	22,135	1,689	221	494	580	201	252
1961	28,493	40,303	25,047	28,150	1,471	214	497	580	211	244
1962	30,274	46,030	26,369	29,866	1,402	233	531	616	240	267
1963	35,048	52,283	29,079	32,316	1,487	268	534	646	252	281
1964	39,482	56,367	31,770	33,969	1,645	440	569	701	264	312
1965	39,382	62,208	34,852	39,663	1,771	339	614	758	254	354
1966	44,158	61,865	37,508	38,950	1,828	334	662	821	253	438

Sources: Rocznik Statystyczny, 1964, p. 301; Rocznik Statystyczny, 1965, p. 313; Rocznik Statystyczny, 1967, p. 328.

[a] Does not include registered letters.